Runes for Beginners:

A complete Guide to Norse Divination, Reading Elder Futhark Runes,Magic Spells, Rituals,and Symbols

Hans Niklas Hellström

Table of Contents

INTRODUCTION

Norse magic in your life can take many forms. It might be as simple as casting a simple spell, or it could be a complex ritual of runes and pagan beliefs. One thing is for sure, though - magic gives your life and soul purpose and substance.

It may be that you're looking for a way to channel your spiritual side, or perhaps just for an interesting way to navigate the world. Or maybe it is a way to learn about yourself and gain insight into your inner thoughts. It is an activity with no strings attached but is still quite special and unique in its own right. The search isn't easy, as many things must go right before the magic can be used effectively.

Many people can tap into the power of magic, but only an elite few are successful at it. The key is to breathe life into your craft and ask your gods for guidance. Your magic will reveal itself eventually, but only after you learn how to make it happen.

The magic of the Norse people is very specific when it comes to what it hopes to accomplish. It's not simply a practice used for good, but one that seeks to bring only harm to their enemies. This means that you need to ask yourself if your intentions are pure before even considering starting down this path for you to learn this kind of magic. Norse magic is hugely influenced by the concept of fate, whether concerning a person's specific destiny or affecting it. Its practitioners view it as a way to examine and perhaps exert some control over one's fate, but it is not used to change it.

And, whether through written symbols or chanted words that represent those symbols, Norse magic is also devoted to the idea of being able to manifest one's desires. This manifestation process is related primarily to the practice of galdr. Runes are the key to the practice of galdr.

We are starting as beginners, but there's no better place or time than this to bring the power of Norse magic into our lives.

Runes are an ancient, mysterious alphabet that is used for casting spells and divination. Often believed to be some secret magic, they were most commonly found on magical amulets and breastplates. Runes are often seen as a key component in the practice of Norse religion and spirituality. Runes can be used in many ways in the modern-day, too.

You may find them enchanting for their unique and often cryptic nature, or you may wish to practice divination with them. You can just experiment and see what runes are proper for you.

The practice of Norse magic emphasizes using good and evil, the positive and the negative. The Norse people believed that everything in the universe was alive, which means that they used the energy that flows through them to help their welfare. This energy is called "líf" or life force within Norse magic circles.

This practice is based on Norse mythology because it calls upon the gods and goddesses from that period. The people believed that you needed to connect with them to gain their favor and avoid angering them.

The ancient Norse people believed that the elements of nature were divine. This means that they used the ground, air, fire, water, and plants as their primary means of communication for this form of magic.

The Norse people would always consult the elements of nature before they would perform any magic. They believed that everything was alive, including themselves, so they would consult with the gods to learn their ways to gain their favor.

The Norse people made up many spells as part of their magic practice. They used writing and runes—or unique three-sided letters—to perform them. These spells were often repeated to bring about the desired results.

Runes are used in various ways in the ancient Norse magic system. One of the ways that they are used is for communication with spiritual beings. They also help cast spells, give blessings and curses, and bring about signs from other realms.

A person who practices Norse magic believes that there is always a connection between the two worlds when it comes to magic. An example is if a person throws a ball into the air, it will always fall back to earth, and of this, the Norse magic practitioner believes that all things have a connection with the other world as well.

Norse magic practitioners have also used spells to call upon spirits, or ghosts, to communicate with them. Many people have used this practice over the years because they wanted to learn about their future or what their purpose was in life. Let's get started.

CHAPTER 1: THE NORDIC PEOPLES

Norsemen is a term used for the Nordic people who lived in the North Atlantic region of what we know today as Scandinavia (Norway, Denmark, Sweden, and later, Iceland). An Old Norse language was established based on Germanic and Indo-European origins before the Viking Age. Although basic agriculture collapsed by 550 C.E. and was only restored towards the 8th century, historical evidence begins to show us a more detailed picture of set practices and beliefs coinciding with foreign influences. A more controlled paganism, if you will.

Their early society was not technically a literary one, and looking into their lives requires an understanding of their oral tradition, seen in early rune inscriptions and later in the sagas and poems. The stories were told, but the reasons and methods were left for interpretation.

The Norse were predominantly farmers, fishermen, and traders. It is often overlooked that their lifestyles were more than just pillaging and conquering. Their connection with their mythologies and their rituals of magic is rooted heavily in their actual day-to-day lives, rather than it being, for instance, a civilization polarized by different beliefs. They were unified and complex.

The Origins of Norsemen

Vikings came from Sweden, Norway, and Denmark, many hundreds of years before they were recognized as stand-alone countries, and they were mostly land-owning farmers and fishermen. They lived in villages ruled by chieftains or clan leaders, and they had few towns. Chieftains often fought for dominance over the lands, and with a seemingly inexhaustible arsenal of strong men who sought adventure, it was fairly easy for skillful leaders to organize armies and fearful bands. Historians are unsure what prompted Vikings to leave their lands and become seafaring pillagers, but they do propose a couple of theories.

The political instability caused by the frequent clashes between clans makes a good motive for branching out. Another would be localized overpopulation, which led to families owning smaller and smaller lands that could no longer provide sustenance for all the family members. Additionally, around the seventh and eighth centuries, the Vikings refined the way they constructed ships and vessels, adding sails and modifying their structures to sustain longer voyages. These longships were swift and shallow, allowing them to go across the North Sea and land on the beaches of unsuspecting lands. If we consider shipping advances, the troubled socio-economic situation of the Vikings at the time, the adventurous nature of these warrior-spirited people, and the tales of riches brought along by merchants, it's not hard to understand why one day they decided to raid the coasts of Europe.

The first historical account of a Viking classical hit-and-run raid dates back to the year 793, when a monastery in Lindisfarne, England was plundered of its sacred, golden religious artifacts. Though, as a side note here, it is unlikely that this was the first time the Vikings attacked England. Evidence shows that English coastal villages had started to organize defenses against sea attacks earlier in the eighth century, suggesting that there were Viking raids or at least attempts before the attack on the Lindisfarne monastery. Many medieval English documents refer to them as "seagoing pagans" for their tendency to target holy places, which, to be fair, were full of unarmed men and gold, so who can blame the Vikings for taking the opportunity? The term "Viking," which is derived from the old Scandinavian word *vikingir* (pirate) or from the word *vik,* which means "bay," was popularized closer to the end of the historical Viking Age. Terms such as *Dani* (inhabitants of present Denmark), *Normani* (Northmen), and simply *pagani* (pagans) were more generally used when referring to the Scandinavian warriors by the European people who were unlucky enough to face their wrath.

From the year 793 forwards, Viking bands consisting of freemen, retainers, and young, adventure-seeking men led by chieftains had gone on to further attack England and its surroundings, especially Scotland, Ireland, and France. Additionally, some accounts from the latter years of the Viking Era speak of Viking attacks or sightings in the Iberian Peninsula, Ukraine, Russia, and even the Byzantine Empire. Originally, the raids were pretty small-scale. There were only a handful of ships, and the Vikings would happily return home when they collected enough booty or if they encountered a resilient defense. But from the 850s, the Vikings began to double down on the force and organization of their raids, establishing bases in the newly conquered lands and starting to dominate the surrounding island areas.

During the Bronze Age, the Celts and Vikings were the largest groups to inhabit the northern world, and the fusion between the two was inevitable. The Celts inhabited northern England, Scotland, and Ireland but also spread to Northern Italy and Spain. Some think that due to similarity in language and culture there is a genetic connection between Vikings and Celts. The truth of the matter is that they were equally influenced by each other but had no genetic correlation. Celtic people were not seafarers and were more oriented toward growing their own lands than pillaging others.

The Celts and ancient Germanic people were neighbors before they decided to migrate and settle in separate lands during the Dark Ages. The Celts took to Ireland and Scotland from their Indo-European and Anatolian migration while the Germanic people mostly settled in Scandinavia.

During the Viking Age, the Celts had more influence on the

Vikings in culture and language as they were already Christianized by the 5th century, whereas the Vikings contributed riches and the contact with foreign goods from trades. The Vikings landed in Ireland around the 7th century after having had some practice raiding and pillaging in East England and Scotland. They were incredibly important in the foundation of some major Irish towns known today, like Dublin and Cork. This clearly tells us that there was not solely violence, but some diplomacy and shared trade too.

Ancient Celtic tribes did not invent their own runic language; it was adopted from the Norse influence before and during the migrations, where both feuds and social interactions took place.

These people were a mix of Norsemen and people from Ireland, called the Gaelic. When the Viking Age was in full bloom around the 9th century, the settlers that arrived in Ireland and Scotland interbred with the local people, adopting language and customs. Leaving behind the Norse gods and converting to Christianity was termed Gaelicization. This meant that their culture was altered to such a degree in influence over a few generations that they considered themselves more Gaelic than Norse.

Even after the conversion and after the Norse-Gaels disappeared entirely as a people, they still left a long-lasting history in Ireland and Scotland. For instance, many Irish towns bear Norse-Gaelic names and the Scottish gallowglass warmongers were descendants of these people.

Norse Religion

Just like all complex religions, Norse spirituality had two main elements: rituals and mystical knowledge that allowed people to understand the inner workings of the universe and how to find their purpose.

When it comes to rituals and other practical ways of worshipping the deities we don't have much to refer to. It is obvious that the Norse gods had a devout religious following which served the social, spiritual, and psychological needs of the Vikings, but the myths and legends do little to explain how the actual worship of the gods played out. Historical evidence speaks of the Norse *blot*, a ceremony through which Odin and other important deities were celebrated. The blots were usually performed at temples or special "blot houses" and they involved sacrifices, of both the human and animal kind. Enemy rulers or noblemen were frequently sacrificed to honor

Odin, while animals were used wherever the specific deity had an animal that they could be linked to, such as Freyr with boars. The animals would be killed and consumed by the religious practitioners, in a ceremony that somewhat resembles a modern Christian communion - meaning that the animal was seen as an embodiment of God.

Blots were a central part of Vikings' lives, and the month of November was named after the divine ceremonies "Blotmonth" or "Bloodmonth." Old Anglo-Saxon writings speak of en masse sacrifices of cattle and horses, where the blood was gathered in special vessels to be consumed and "splashed" over the attendees of the ceremonies. A priest would then bless the meat, vessels, and goblets used at the feast and they would ensure the celebrations. A goblet was ceremoniously emptied to honor certain gods. First Odin, to bless the ruling class, then Freya and Freyr to bring peace and good harvest. Attendees could also empty a goblet to honor their departed.

Viking sacrifices were seen as gifts to the gods, to show appreciation for their blessings and for maintaining order and peace in the cosmos. For the Norsemen, their deities were not perfect or all-powerful. They too were governed by fate and by the laws of the world. Vikings saw them first and foremost as protectors of order, that kept the evil forces in check and seldomly intervened in the events that happened in the mortal world. If we consider how dangerous and harsh the Viking world was, it's not hard to see why the Christian portrayal of a loving and omnipotent God didn't flourish in the minds and hearts of Norsemen. They worshipped their gods with the hopes that they would, in exchange, bless and protect their families and communities. That was all.

Most of the mystic knowledge of the Vikings came from their myths and legends. Through these tales of the realm of the gods and how the cosmos came to be, the Norsemen can easily find ideals, role models, and goals to strive towards in their lives. Odin is a model for kings, knowledge seekers, and fathers alike. Thor is the ultimate Viking - warrior, loyal, and determined to fulfill his duty to the very end. Freya and Frigg are symbols of motherhood, the joy of life, and Norse magic. Freyr is the personification of wealth, peace, and prosperity. And the symbolic peace that is established between the Aesir and the Vanir tells Vikings that all the aspects that the deities represent and equally important to lead a happy life and have a successful society. Norse tales are also full of numerology and hidden elements that only the wise and knowledgeable can decipher. These people who were wise enough to see beyond the apparent could practice divination and seidr, to foresee and influence someone's fate.

There's no doubt that Viking spirituality ran deep, and was a lot more complex than Anglo-Saxons of the time believed. And yet, close to the end of the Viking Age, the Norsemen started to give up on their gods and traditions and embrace Christianity. There are many dramatized stories speaking of forced conversions and even of saints or angels that aided Christian clerics in their mission to bring God to the Viking pagans. But in reality, Christianity came to the Viking world naturally and progressively. Vikings were very flexible with their beliefs, and they started to incorporate Christian elements in their religion as soon as they set foot on European soil. Sure, there were a few traditionalists who clung to their Mjolnir pendants, but most of the Scandinavian population was open to inclusion, though they opted to accept one element at a time rather than make a full 180 degrees conversion. Old Norse iconography mixed with Christian symbols and customs to create hybrid religions. It was perfectly acceptable for baptized Norsemen to still invoke Thor's protection in their times of need.

The conversion to Christianity of the Norse population was slow, and it started way before Christian missionaries officiated it. The challenge clerics had was not to teach Norsemen the values and practices of Christianity, but rather to convince them to embrace only these Christian elements, and give up on all remnants of their pagan beliefs. The conversion to Christianity didn't happen on its own as a singular event. It came together with the "Europeanization" of Vikings, which led to the Norsemen giving up on traditional values and norms. They made the switch from chieftains to kings, they adopted the Latin alphabet, and little by little the Viking world adhered to European standards.

But what triggered the conversion to Christianity, in the first place? Well, although we can't know for sure, the most plausible reason is the selfish character of the Vikings. Remember, they worshipped their gods in hopes of garnering protection, blessings, and prosperity. But there were things the Norse gods could not provide. Norse deities were ambivalent and not prone to forgive. They did not offer the salvation of one's soul, and they were not always in the "mood" to listen to mere mortals. The Christian God, however, was kind, ever-loving, and forgiving. For the Vikings, all that mattered was who could offer more, thus Christianity was an easy pick. The benefits that it bought were deemed enough to merit worship and loyalty. Viking kings and rulers were usually the first to convert because it helped them make powerful alliances. And if the king went first, his people would usually follow. As time went by, Christianity slowly became the default, and the once pagan Vikings became devout followers of God.

CHAPTER 2: THE CREATION OF THE WORLD

The world began, as it would end, in the fire. From the primordial chaos which held neither day nor night, sea nor land, life nor death, a spark arose. The flame, feeding on its own hunger, raged and spread and became the bright hot world of Muspelheim, a living furnace that poured rivers of fire and blasts of hot air into the surrounding void.

Once heat and light existed, their opposites also came into being. Across the universe from Muspelheim another world took shape: Niflheim, icebound, dark and deadly cold. From Niflheim, a venomous chilling wind poured into the void and a slow river of grinding ice.

Ice and fire met in the emptiness. There were terrible explosions, and the void was filled with flying sparks and shards of shattered ice, with fountains of water and jets of steam. That collision birthed the frost-giant Ymir. He was strong and cold and deadly as the breath of Niflheim, but he had the fire-spark of life in him. Ymir sweated as the sparks flew around him, and from the sweat-drops, new giants came to life.

Ymir and his brood were not the only ones born of the ice-melt. The cow Audhumbla also took shape between fire and ice, and Ymir and his children drank her milk. She also was thirsty, and she quenched her thirst by licking the ice. Something new began to emerge under the strokes of her tongue: first what looked like a man's hair emerged, and then a head, and then the whole figure stepped free of the ice and looked about him. His name was Buri, and he was the first of the gods. Buri was as beautiful as he was strong, and he wanted others of his own kind. He made his own son, Borr. Borr loved the giantess Bestla, and she bore sons, of whom the greatest was Odin.

Odin and his brothers fought Ymir. The war was remembered long after the reasons were forgotten. Maybe the giant didn't approve of his offspring marrying gods instead of one another. Maybe both Odin and Ymir wanted to claim the whole world for their own people. Be that as it may, they fought, and Odin and his brothers won. Ymir fell dead in the void between the world of fire and the world of ice, and Ymir's blood rose in a great flood and drowned the other frost-giants—all but the giant Bergelmir and his wife. While the others fought, Bergelmir had built a great ship, and as the flood rose, he and his wife went into their ship and rode the blood-tide to a safe place beyond the reach of the young gods.

Odin and his brothers turned from fighting to the building. They took Ymir's body and reshaped it into a world, a flat ring set midway between the worlds of ice and fire, in a place of flowing water and mild air. Ymir's icy blood became the world's lakes and seas, his flesh and bones the land and the mountains. His skull was set up above the world, becoming the arch of the sky. The gods took fire from the sparks of Muspelheim and threw them into the air beneath that arch to give light to the world. On the outer margins of that world, besides the endless sea that marked its boundary, was a wasteland inhabited by Bergelmir's children and their children, the giants who remembered Ymir's death and waited for their chance to avenge it. But in the middle of the world, the gods raised a defensive wall, built from Ymir's eyebrows, to keep the giants at bay. This defended land was called Midgard, the world of men.

Here, after chaos and war, there was rest and order and the beginning of another kind of life. The sun warmed the earth. Green plants sprang up and grew. Odin and his brothers took two trees, shaped them in the image of the gods, breathed life into their flesh and inspiration into their souls.

Ask was the first man, and Embla the first woman, and from those two came all the people of the world.

The gods also took the maggots that gnawed Ymir's flesh, gave them a humanlike form, and breathed wisdom into them. These became the race of dwarves, who shared the world with humans, not always happily... As we shall see in other tales.

How the First Gods Were Born

Ymir and the giants weren't alone. The melted ice that made Ymir also made a cow, Audhumla, who ate a salt-lick that came from the ice that was still dripping. When she got to the bottom of the salt-lick, there was a person! This person was named Buri, the very first Aesir, which is a tribe of gods.

Buri had a son named Borr (sometimes spelled Bor), who married the daughter of one of the giants that came from Ymir. Borr and his wife, Bestla, were the parents of Odin. Since Borr was almost a God and Bestla was a giant, Odin was half-god and half-giant. This made him fit to be the chief of the Aesir tribe.

Odin also had two brothers, Vili and Ve. Together, the three of them made the rest of the world, including the sky, land, plants, oceans, and clouds.

Ymir (the Screamer), the first living creature, born in Ginnungagap from the melted ice of Niflheim, was a giant and a force of destruction. He was also a hermaphrodite who could reproduce on his own. As he slept, the giant started to sweat, and from the sweat of his armpits, a man and a woman were born, while from the sweat of his legs emerged another man. This is how the first frost giants were born into this world. From the ice that was still melting in the void, another creature was brought into being - the cow Audhumla. She would lick salty ice blocks for nourishment and she graciously offered her rivers of milk for Ymir to feast on and grow.

While liking the salt, Audhumla found and uncovered a man - Buri (the Progenitor), the first of the Aesir gods. Buri was a strong handsome man, and he had a son called Bor. He then married Besla, the daughter of a frost giant. This unlikely pair of Gods and giants had three children: Odin, Vili, and Ve.

The Creation of Humans

One day, Bor's sons were strolling along the beach and they found two logs—one from an ash tree and one from an elm tree. From each log, they fashioned a human being, one male and one female. Odin gave them life and a lively spirit, Vili gifted them shape, speech, feelings, and five senses, and Vé endowed them with movement, mind, and intelligence. The man was named Ask, and the woman was named Embla. "From these two descend the whole human race whose assigned dwelling was within Midgard."

A man called Mundilfari quickly caused the gods some chagrin. He had two children who were breathtakingly lovely to look on. He named his gentle and graceful daughter Sol (sun) and the striking and handsome son Mani (moon).

The gods, finding this very presumptuous, placed the children in the heavens. Sol was commanded to drive the horses Arvak (Early Rising) and Alsvid (Very Fast) who pulled the chariot of the sun, which the gods had made to give light to the Earth, across the sky. Her brother Mani was told to guide the passage of the moon and control its waxing and waning.

CHAPTER 3: THE NORSE PANTHEON

The Norse had a concept of deities that expressed more than just omnipotence and fear, but also knowledge and kindness. These gods inspire countless myths and folktales around creation and destruction. Each having a specific character reference and theme, they were more than ethereal powers in another reality, but real flesh and blood beings that directly affected their everyday lives.

The word pantheon can be understood as a collective group of gods within a particular culture; for example, the Egyptian pantheon or the Greek pantheon would consist of those regions' collective Gods.

The Norse pantheon consisted of the Aesir, Vanir, jötnar, and many other minor deities and demigods. Thus, the Norse pantheon consisted of a wide range of deities and divine beings responsible for and controlled different sectors of the nine realms of the cosmos.

However, the list of the Norse pantheon is incredibly lengthy and is made up of many different bloodlines and races, making it difficult to single out every Norse God of the time. Thus, to truly grasp the Norse pantheon, it is best to highlight only the most important gods and goddesses that the Norsemen worshipped during the Viking age.

The Norse pantheon can be divided into three major groups. These groups consist of the Aesir (the newest generation of gods), the Vanir (the old gods), and the jötnar (the giants who inhabited the universe first). However, only the most important of these gods. After years of bloodshed between these three groups, the Aesir would come out victorious and be the most powerful gods who would rule the cosmos. The various gods were depicted differently depending on who wrote it, sometimes adding or removing certain characteristics of their theme and influence. The alteration is best seen in the aspects and powers of the female deities' beings transferring into that of male deities, centralizing the worship in patriarchal figures. Even more, the various names given to the gods and realms are sometimes changed or altered with a literature largely more descriptive and narrative than its earlier works.

THE AESIR GODS AND GODDESSES

Odin

Odin is the king of all Aesir gods and ruler of Asgard. He is known by many names which include Gangleri, Odinn, Othinn, Vak, and Valtam. Odin, also called the Allfather, is the Lord of War, Death and Knowledge.

He is also associated with the gallows, healing, magic, poetry, royalty, shamanism, sorcery, wisdom, and the runic alphabet. Wednesday is derived from his name (Woden's day).

Odin was born to Borr and Bestla. Borr was the son of Buri, the first Norse God while Bestla was the daughter of the giant Bölthorn. Buri was formed when the cow Audhumbla licked the salty ice of Ginnungagap to survive while she was feeding Ymir, the first frost giant.

The All-knowing Allfather of the Gods is married to Frigg though he also had dalliances with Freya and Rind, among others. Odin sired Baldr, Hodr and Hermod with Frigg while he had Thor with Jord and Vidar with Grid. He is also the father of Viðarr and Váli. In another account (by Snorri Sturluson), Odin is also the father of Bragi, Heimdallr, Höd and Týr although other versions stress, they, particularly

Týr, were sired by someone else.

Thor

Everyone knows about the superhero Thor, but the Norse God Thor is a little bit different. He is the son of Odin and Jord, who was a giant. This makes Thor a giant too, since his father is half-giant.

Thor is the God of thunder. He is the perfect example of an ideal warrior. Every Viking looked up to Thor. He is courageous, strong, and a loyal defender of Asgard.

While Thor also had a belt that gave him strength, his most famous possession is his hammer, Mjöllnir, which means "lightning." The lightning hammer used by the thunder God is one way the Norse explained thunderstorms. When you hear thunder and see lightning, it's Thor riding on a chariot in the sky, slaying giants.

Since Thor is the God of thunder, he also has some power over rain. The Norse believed he could help their crops grow by controlling the weather.

Tyr

Tyr is considered a minor God in Norse mythology but before the Age of the Vikings, he was deemed the highest of all gods. Tyr is also known as Teiws, Tiw, T'waz, Cyo, Tius, Tio, and Ziu.

Tyr is ultimately the continuation of Dyeus, the archetypal father God of the Proto-Indo-European period. He was the father of the gods before Odin came into the picture. Other versions of his story say that Tyr is actually the son of Odin. Tyr was also the original Norse God of War. When the Vikings took over during the Migration Age, Tyr's popularity took a hit and he was supplanted by Odin and Thor. It is believed that the Vikings did not espouse the characteristics of Tyr which were more of bravery and courage on the battlefield.

Gefjun

The Gefion Fountain in Copenhagen, Denmark, designed by Danish artist Anders Bundgaard in 1908, and is attributed to Prose Edda.

Gefjun's (or Gefion) name means "giver" or "generous one," which is exactly who she is. She is the goddess of abundance and agriculture. Most of the stories with Gefjun talk about her helping farmers and making sure the land is ready to grow crops.

Baldr

The son of Odin and Frigg, Baldr was one of the most revered Asgardian gods. He was the God of Light, Beauty, and Happiness. Baldr, known also as Balder and Baldur, was married to Nanna with whom he had Nep and Forseti. Baldr resided at Breidablik.

Baldr has always dreamt of dying and his mother, concerned with his visions, asked everyone and everything to not cause harm to her son. But the jealous Loki would not have any of that.

He disguised himself and tricked Frigg into revealing Baldr's only weakness — the mistletoe. Frigg, during her quest to make every creature and object to take the oath of not hurting Baldr, deemed it unnecessary to ask the same from the small mistletoe.

Sif

The Norse Corn or Maize Goddess and wife of Thor, Sif was the Goddess of Harvest.

Sif is portrayed by Jaimie Alexander in the *Thor* movie franchise. Unlike the black-haired character in the movie, the goddess Sif had golden hair. Her hair is important because it would be the subject of some trouble that brewed between brothers Thor and Loki.

The mischievous Loki sneaked into Sif's room and cut off her glorious hair. Because of this, Sif was extremely distraught which caused the earth to be barren and crops to not grow. Of course, her husband was furious and pummeled Loki until he relented in setting things straight. Loki convinced the dwarf brothers, the Sons of Ivaldi, to make a new set of golden hair for Sif.

Bragi

Bragi was the Eloquent God of Poetry and Music. This son of Odin and Frigg was also a patron of the poets. Bragi was married to Iðunn, daughter of Ivald and the Goddess of Youth and Apples.

He is often depicted as a man with a long white beard holding a golden harp and has runes carved on his tongue.

He welcomed fallen warriors to Valhalla with his music.

One story says that Bragi was originally a real person named Bragi Boddason. He lived during the 9th century.

It was believed that he was a well-known and well-loved skald or poet of his generation that his fellow skalds added him in Norse mythology and made him a God.

Idun

Idun is the goddess that carries the fruits of immortality that let the gods stay young and live (almost) forever. The best-known story about Idun is one where she has kidnapped thanks to Loki.

Loki got into a fight with a giant disguised as an eagle. The eagle eventually grabbed Loki and started to fly away with him. Loki wanted the eagle to put him back on the ground, but the eagle said he wouldn't do it unless Loki brought the goddess Idun to him. What the eagle really wanted was the fruit of immortality. To save himself, Loki said he would bring Idun.

Loki tricked Idun into leaving Asgard by telling her there were fruits better than hers outside the city's walls. When she left the safety of Asgard, the eagle took her.

Vidar

The Wide-Ruling One, Vidar is also known as Vidarr, Vithar, and Vitharr. The God of Vengeance and Silence was sired by Odin by Grior. He was prophesized as the one who will avenge the death of Odin during the Ragnarok by stabbing Fenrir right in the heart.

Other accounts say Vidar killed the wolf by stepping on its lower jaw and pulling up the upper jaw ripping it apart. This is why Vidar has been known for his thick shoe made of leather pieces from the shoes given by Midgardians throughout time.

Vidar's vengeance happened after the swelling sea and the fire from Surtr subsided and allowed the "Silent God" to proceed with his destined task.

Sigyn

Sigyn is Loki's wife. There aren't a lot of stories about her, but there is one that shows how much she loved Loki.

After Loki convinced one of the other gods to kill Baldur (accidentally), the rest of the gods punished him. They tied him down in a cave and put a snake that dripped venom over him. To stop the venom from hitting Loki, Sigyn sat next to him with a bowl to catch the venom.

Höd

Hod, Hodr, Hoder and Hodur. Like the other gods, the blind God was known by different variations of his name. He was son to Odin and Frigg and twin brother to the much-loved Baldr. He was the God of Winter and Darkness.

Baldr was killed by Hod after Loki tricked him. As punishment, Hod was killed by Vali, the child of Odin and Rindr who was born for the sole purpose of avenging Baldr.

Forseti

Forseti was the son of Baldr and Nanna. He was the God of Justice and Reconciliation and was known as "the presiding one" for holding court disputes in his hall and paving the way for reconciliation between opposing individuals or factions.

Forseti dwells in Glitnir where his house is made of a silver roof supported by gold pillars that gave off a bright light seen from far away. He was closely related to the practice of meditation.

Frigg

Frigg is Odin's wife and the highest-ranking goddess in Asgard. She practices a type of magic called seidr, which involves learning about the future and changing it, if possible. Some Norse women practice seidr, and they would sometimes perform magic in exchange for food or a place to sleep. Frigg's name means "beloved" and she represents love and marriage.

Vili and Ve

Vili's name means "will," and he is sometimes called the God of motivation. When Vili, Ve, and Odin made the first humans, Vili gave them the ability to think and feel.

Ve's name means "temple." He is the God of the sacred, which means anything that has to do with the gods. After Vili gave the first humans the gifts of thinking and feeling, Ve gave them speech, sight, and hearing.

Loki

Loki is famously known as the trickster God. While most of the other gods like and take care of each other, Loki is the outcast.

He goes back and forth between helping the gods and helping the giants. Loki's popularity, or notoriety, within the stories that make up the corpus of Norse mythology, has extended to members of his family and kin group as well.

According to the stories, Loki was the son of the Jötunn Fárbauti and a female named Laufey. Some scholars think that Laufey might have been a member of the Aesir; this may help explain the fact that Loki is frequently given the additional epithet "Laufeyjarson." His mother's blood may also have been his entree into the halls where the other gods and goddesses lived. On the other hand, Loki's association with fire may have been inherited from his father Fárbauti. Loki's brothers are named Helblindi and Býleistr.

In contrast to the uncertainty surrounding his parents, there is more definite information to be found on Loki's spouse and offspring. His wife, Sigyn, is a member of the Aesir and seems to be determined to stay by her husband's side no matter how he might aid or attack the rest of the pantheon. She bears Loki's two sons, whose names are variously given as Váli (the same as one of the sons of Odin), Narfi, and Nari.

He can be playful and funny, but most of the time he's not a nice guy. In many of the stories about Loki, his tricks get him into trouble. One of these stories is about the making of Thor's hammer.

Thor had a wife named Sif. She had beautiful, long golden hair. One day when Loki was bored, he decided to cut off Sif's hair. Thor was very mad and threatened to beat up Loki. To stop Thor from hurting him, Loki promised to have a new head of hair made for Sif. He went to Nidavellir, the home of the dwarves, to have the head of hair made.

Dwarves were the best craftsmen, and they were able to make new hair for Sif. They also made a ship named Skidbladnir that could fold up to the size of a pocket and a mighty spear called Gungnir.

Heimdall

Another one of Odin's sons,Heimdall the God of Light and Protection, is known for his gift of foresight. He also has a keen sense of sight and hearing. In fact, he can see s far as a hundred miles whether it is bright or dark.

He also goes by Gullintani, a name derived from his golden teeth. He was the son of nine mothers born at the end of the world. Heimdall has a hall in Himinbjorg where he saw the onset of Ragnarok.

Heimdall is tasked with guarding the Bifrost against the intruder, particularly the giants.

His home is on top of the Bifrost so he is always there to watch over it. He seldom sleeps, he can see as well as a bird can, and he can hear very well, too. Heimdall holds the horn called Gjallarhorn, which he only uses to let the gods of Asgard know when there are intruders.

He owns the Gjallarhorn and rides Gulltopp, a horse with a golden mane. He fathered the different races of mankind –

serfs, peasants, and warriors -- while he was the God Rig. Heimdall died during the Ragnarok but not before killing Loki.

VANIR GODS AND GODDESSES

Njord

Njord is both a member of the Vanir and Aesir tribes of gods. He is actually from Vanir but was sent to the Aesirs as a hostage (along with his children) during the war between the tribes. Njord was the God of the Wind and Sea.

He was often called upon by seafarers for a safe passage. The Vanir God is associated with fertility and wealth.

He fathered Freyr and Freya by Nerthus (in some accounts). He was married for a short time to the giantess Skadi. The giantess came to the gods to seek revenge for the death of her father Thzaji who was killed while Iðunn was being rescued from him.

Freya

She was known to have the ability to control desires and was the most popular völva or shamanic seer. Loki once accused Freya of having affairs with all the gods and elves which may be accurate due to the goddess' tendency to seek pleasure.

Freyja was also made an honorary member of the Aesir tribe along with her father and brother. Freya was often confused with Frigga who is identical to her. She was married to Odr (who was identical to Odin) with whom she had daughters Hnoss and Gersemi.

The goddess presides over Fólkvangr where half of the warriors who die in battle go. She dwells in her hall Sessrúmnir.

Ull

Ull was the God of Justice. He was also known as a multi-talented God as he was the patron of archery, skiing, and dueling aside from being an excellent hunter. Ull, also named Oller, Uller, Ullr, Valder and Vuldr, was born to Sif while his father is believed by some to be Egill-Örvandill.

Egill was a renowned archer from whom Ull obviously took after. He dwells in Ydalir. While many consider Ull to be part of the Aesir tribe, some believe that he originated from the Vanirs.

Ull was described as a beautiful being with the

characteristics of a great warrior. It is believed that Ull was a great wizard who used a magic bone for traveling particularly for traversing the sea.

Ull took over Odin when the Lord of Asgard was exiled for ten years. He was also involved with the elves of Völundarkviða as some believe.

Odr

Nothing is known about Odr other than that he is just like Odin, but he rules the Vanir instead of the Aesir. He also has a daughter named Hnoss.

Freyr

Freyr might be a Vanir god, but he is supposedly good friends with the Aesir tribe, too. He was a very well-loved God to the Norse people. Freyr brings wealth, peace, good health, and good harvests.

Freyr lives in Alfheim with the elves instead of in Vanir with the other gods of his tribe. When Loki brought back Thor's hammer along with all the other gifts from the dwarves, Freyr received the ship Skidbladnir and the boar Gullinbursti.

Nerthus

Nerthus is Njord's sister and represents Mother Earth. She is a goddess who likes peace, and the people who worshipped her would lock up all their weapons for a few days when they thought she would visit their homes or villages. Besides her love of non-violence, nothing else is really known about Nerthus.

JÖTNAR

Variously translated as "ettin" or, more commonly, "giant," the term Jötnar (Jötun in the singular) refers to those beings who live beneath or among rocks. Typically, giants are thought of as repulsive beingsThese supernatural beings of the natural world have, from the beginning of time, been the arch-rivals of the Æsir and Vanir. Although they often appear as the adversaries of the Aesir, in some stories, they are actually the victims of unprovoked attacks by the gods, while in others, they are able to win victories over those same gods.

The Jötun live in the icy realm of Jötunheim, which is closely connected to Midgard by mountain ranges and dense forests, while the fire giants live in Múspellsheimr, their realm of fire. They are the catalyst of the great ending in Ragnarök, setting fire to the tree Yggdrasil and ending everything in flame.

Different types of giants appear in the stories: there are clay-giants, fire-giants, mountain-giants, sea-giants, wind-giants, and frost-giants. Sometimes, these giants display the characteristics of their homes and lairs, such as Surtr who seems to be capable of generating or controlling fire. Others, such as Aegir and his wife Rán, live on an island in a hall next to the waves and are thus described as sea-giants.They represented the original nature of chaos and destruction in comparison to God's representing life and order.

Aegir and Ran

Aegir is God of the Ocean and ruled all creatures of the sea. He is married to Ran, Goddess of the Sea and mother of the nine billow maidens who are considered the spirits of the waves.

Both belong to the race of jotunns or giants who have long been at odds with the Aesir gods. The two, however, are friends with the Asgardian deities. The giants regularly invite them to their feasts. While Aegir was known as a gracious host, Ran was the opposite.

She was mostly responsible for capsizing ships and drowning sailors then having them live in their underwater kingdom.

Hel

Another giantess, Hel is the Goddess of Death and the Underworld. Her realm was known as Helheim or Hel in which those who died of sickness and old age dwelled.

She was born from the union of Loki and the giantess Angrboda. The wolf Fenrir and the serpent Jormungand are her siblings according to the version of Snorri who many feel is inaccurate.

As a matter of fact, many scholars view Hel as a literary creation of scholars and poets before them. Like their father Loki, the three siblings were prophesized to bring trouble and tragedy.

MYTHICAL CREATURES

Trolls

Some tales from Sweden describe trolls as monstrous beings with many heads who can either live in the forest and mountains or caves. The first kind of trolls that live in the mountains are known to be large, aggressive, stupid, and slow beings, always getting outwitted by the hero in the story. Those that live in caves are shy and seen as shorter than humans with stumpy arms and legs but with a fair amount of intelligence. They use the environment around them to influence their power or protect themselves and hide. These creatures emerged into mythology from the idea of the giants (jötun) in their cosmology and realms, as the word troll in Old Norse is *jätte*.

Dwarfs

It's hard to imagine Thor without his trusty hammer Mjölnir in his hand, or Odin without his spear Gungnir; likewise, Freyja's beauty is completed and complemented by the fabulous jewel Brísingamen. What do these items have in common? They were all created by the race of metalsmiths and craftsmen known as the dwarfs. Different groups or families of dwarfs are responsible for different mythical items, from the unbreakable ribbon or binding called Gleipnir, to the items in the possession of the God Freyr (his boar and his ship).

The *Poetic* and *Prose Edda*s differ somewhat on the origin of dwarfs, as while both books say that they sprang forth from Ymir's body, the former says that they were spontaneously generated from the giant's blood and bones. The latter, on the other hand, says that the dwarfs were mindless parasites embedded in the giant's flesh and were granted reason by the Aesir. The names of various dwarfs are listed in both books, some being more notable than most. Four, in particular, named Norðri (North), Suðri (South), Austri (East), and Vestri (West), are given the specific task of holding up the sky.

Norns

Not quite goddesses, not quite giants or dwarfs, not quite human – the Norns are identified primarily as female beings, whose primary function is to foresee and govern the destinies of all living things, from the Aesir on down.

The Norns are not actually limited to the trio of Urd, Verdandi, and Skuld; there are many others, who are said to appear around a child when it is newly born, and foretell what that child's destiny will be. Accordingly, some Norns are perceived to be benevolent, while others are malevolent.

Dísir

While the dísir are also said to be female spirits that govern the fates of individuals and families, the primary difference seems to be that they may have been derived from the collective spirits of the family's ancestors. They function as protective spirits, looking after the destinies of their descendants. Festivals were held to honor these spirits, at which sacrifices were made and prayers were said to invoke their favorable regard.

Humans

According to material in the *Poetic Edda*, the first man was named "Ask" and the first woman was named Embla. Their names are derived from trees: "Ask" from the ash tree, and "Embla" from either the elm or a vine. The stories of their creation vary from account to account; some say that it was Odin, Hönir, and Lothur who gave them important gifts, while others say that the three gods involved were Odin and his brothers Vili and Vé.

Elves

The elves, as from the many references we have in popular culture today, are known to be fair, beautiful, and tall beings that are swift in battle and powerful with magic. Initially, in pre-Christian myths, these demi-gods were one class of being who lived in one realm. Later, their mythology developed and they were divided into Light Elves (Ljösáfar) that lived in the realm of Alfheim reigned by the God Freyr, and the Dark Elves (Dökkálfar) that lived deep within the earth and had a darker complexion. Elves were known to cause illness to the humans and, when offered something in return, they could heal them too. Humans were known to also become elves after they died due to the connection of the worship of ancestors to the worship of elves.

CHAPTER 4: RELIGIOUS PRACTICES IN ORIGIN

The ancient people who practiced the Germanic pagan religion often held their rituals in or near bodies of water like lakes, bogs, and marshes. They believed that such places are sacred and can let the mortals contact the divine. It is the reason archaeologists find numerous wooden figures in these locations depicting people with strongly emphasized sexual features, suggesting that they were offerings to the Norse pagan gods of fertility.

Sacrifices were fundamental elements of Norse/Germanic religion. The ancient people believed that destroying or sending the sacrifice in a place where humans cannot access them is a surefire way for them to reach their intended deities. The ritual burning or throwing of sacrificial objects into lakes became frequent. Festivals also frequently accompanied these rituals and involved copious amounts of eating and drinking.

Often, carved wooden figurines were used for sacrifice, but there were also times when people were offered to the gods by weighing them down using stones and throwing them into boggy marshes. Most of the time, the victims were purported to be witches who brought misfortune to their community. Peat bogs were the preferred sacrificial altar of sorts because the body would not dissolve and get sent to the other world. Instead, the body was preserved forever in a state in-between our world and the other world.

At other times, the Norse people would offer their beloved weapons to their gods. Oddly enough, you will not find human remains in the places where weapons are offered up to the gods. Often, the weapons used for sacrifice came from the Norse people's slain enemies, and these were usually sent to Odin.

As Norse Paganism originates from long before Christianity became widespread in Europe, this type of religion is significantly different from that and many other religions. This difference is reflected in the reasons behind followers celebrating their holidays and festivals. Not to mention the distinct way these festivities are carried out. Instead of being a centralized belief system led by priests, Norse Paganism is based on honoring and worshiping gods, whose personas change from one geographical area to another. Despite this, all of these belief systems have one thing in common. They are all related to everyday events and one-time events that have some sort of value to their followers. Furthermore, all Norse pagan rituals are linked to these events and the gods they honor. Moreover, they are extremely important to the entire community, not just to the individuals who live in those communities.

Each holiday is honored by a particular ritual carried out by a person who has a higher function in the community. In ancient times, these persons used to be kings and leaders of one village or groups of villages. Nowadays, this role belongs to either the head of the household or the spiritual head of the Asatru community. The rituals are often accompanied by a sacrifice, or blot - as it's called amongst Asatruars. This sacrifice usually involves killing an animal, removing its blood, and offering it to the gods. This is followed by boiling its meat and sharing it between members of the community. This is the pagan way of worshipping the gods, which is nowadays almost always done on a local level only. However, in ancient times, Great Blots were very common, and they were celebrated on the national level throughout the territory of Scandinavia. There are also everyday blots in the pagan way of life in general. These can be accomplished through a smaller sacrifice or the use of a simple spell or incantation. They can be performed for wealth, long life, fertility, a safe journey, or anything important to the individual or community. They could bring these benefits to everyone as long as it pleased the gods, who were the source of everything that was asked.

Besides the everyday blots, there are a couple of other notable rituals that were and still are part of the lives of everyone practicing Norse Paganism. One example of this is the ritual of birth and naming of a child, during which followers pray to the Norse goddesses Freya and Frigg. First, galdr-songs are sung to ask the goddesses for a safe and successful birth, and if the child is born and survives nine nights, it's placed on their father's knee and sprinkled with water. During this process, the child is named and joins the family by the blessings of the gods. According to Asatru, this is not only a joyous occasion for the family, but it also means the expansion of the whole society.

Marriage rituals are also significant in Norse Paganism because they represent the beginning of family life and all that is good about having a family. Following the wedding ceremony, a number of small rituals are usually performed. All of this culminates in an elegant wedding feast as well as a blot. This blot will be celebrated in the future for the rest of the family's existence. As with other festivities, the marriage rituals are also done in a way that the married couple and their union earn the gods the blessing. This was particularly vital to accomplish in ancient times when the wedding itself was also a legal unification of two families. And while this may have changed in modern times, Asatruars still find the wedding procedure a spiritually binding contract.

Finally, another ritual held in high esteem by the Norse pagans is that of the burial of their loved ones and funeral ceremonies in general. Followers of Norse Paganism indeed put more significance to the person's present life (and the rewards they can get while still alive). However, this doesn't mean they aren't concerned about life after death. Similar to that of other religions, their funeral rites consist of either a cremation ritual or a burial ceremony. In ancient times, cremation was a more prevalent method to send someone on their last journey. And aside from burning them, it literally involved burying the remains along with a form of transport. Whether it was a horse, a wagon, or even a small boat, it served the purpose of ensuring the dead got to their destination safely. Unfortunately, there isn't too much information about the burial or cremation rituals themselves. But we know that they were doing everything to help make these processes easier for the dead and the living, equally.

Norse Pagan Holidays and Festivals

Unlike today, during ancient Norse times, each year had only two seasons. The first one was Summer, which began around the Spring Equinox, and the Norsemen celebrated its beginning with the festival of Ostara. The other one was Winter, starting with the celebrations of Winter nights after the Autumn Equinox. These two are the most significant holidays, celebrated either locally or nationwide in every Asatru community. Of course, aside from these two, numerous other festivals are held between them, varying from larger ones like Yule to lesser festivities. Some of them are still celebrated with small sacrifices, while others have been reduced to feast among family and friends. Despite this, their traditions have been preserved as some of them are still named Blot, which is a reference to the sacrifice people used to make on these occasions. And while most of them are present in parts of modern paganism in one way or another, not all of them are included in the practices of Asatru. In accordance with the values of Norse

Paganism, they were and are to be held with keeping in mind what feels right for the whole community, and most importantly, its individuals.

Yule

Beginning on the night of the 20th of December, Yule is probably the most known Norse holiday, and for a couple of reasons. First, this date signifies the darkest hours of the year (due to the shortest daylight hours), marking the end of it. The commencement of Yule also means a new beginning, along with the hope of entering into a better year. According to Old Norse tales, Yule marks the return of the God Baldur from the realm of Hel, which will lead to the loosening of winter's grip on Earth, thus beginning to end this cold season. Yule lasts 12 nights and is celebrated by numerous feasts, music, and gift-giving. The name of this holiday originates from the Old Norse word HJOL (which means wheel). This is about the wheel of the year being at its lowest point in preparation to rise anew.

The first night of Yule is called Mother Night, and it usually starts by giving homage to the goddess Frigga and the female ancestral spirits called Disir, for the purpose of honoring all females as the world is being reborn. To make sure this rebirth happens and the Sun will rise again, a traditional vigil is held on this night. The rest of the days and nights are spent celebrating the new beginning by sharing music and food with the community, including the dead. Norse pagan people often use all kinds of baked goods and decorations - like the Yule sun wheel or the Yule tree - to welcome anyone into their life.

Mabon

Being a minor blot, Mabon or Haustblot has fewer records of being celebrated than many others. According to some traditions, it's held around the 22nd of September and represents the end of the harvest season. At this time, people were (and in agricultural communities still are) too busy with collecting and storing their harvest. This means that they didn't have time to prepare full feasts like for other festivities. But they did have smaller-sized sacred ritual feasts, which were made to honor the gods of food harvest – Frey, Nerthus, Iduna, and Njord. Jord was once again given thanks for all her contributions, along with Snotra, goddess of hard work and hospitality. Huldra, the keeper of flocks, is also honored for making it possible to raise the animals and have enough meat and other animal products for the colder months.

For the Asatruar, this is still a joyous festival, which is celebrated by building bonfires, feasting, and dancing on the Autumn Equinox. Having lit these fires as their only light source, families and whole pagan communities often gather and bond together by telling old tales over the flame. Traditionally, this is done to avoid being alone and missing since this was considered dangerous because it meant that the person was exposed to the dangers of the coming season. As the second harvest festival of the season, Mabon is also a time to find reasons to be thankful and celebrate surviving another season of hard work. By gathering into masses, people are able to do all this together, strengthening the spirit of the community.

Winter Nights

Despite signifying the beginning of the unforgiving Winter Season, Winter nights are often characterized as a ceremony of wild abandon. Here, one's ancestors are celebrated and asked for help or advice regarding the coming year. This festival, which runs from the 29th of October to the 1st of November, is thought to be a time to foretell the fates of many people. Animals that were not expected to survive the winter were frequently used for these purposes. They are sacrificed for the community's benefit and to ward off evil spirits. Unlike many other rituals, this is often done by the woman of a family. She is considered the ultimate keeper of the house and her family. So, this way, she can protect her entire home.

On this day, Hela, the goddess of the Dead, and Mordgud, the guardian of the Underworld, are honored as new rulers of the ancestors. Nidhogg, the corpse-eating dragon, was asked to spare them, while Hlin, the goddess of Grief, and Hermod, the messenger of the gods, who walked the road to Hel, were also asked to assist in providing comfort to both the living and the dead. Another common way to celebrate this festival was the hallowing and leaving of the Last Sheaf in the field for Odin to find it. He can then bring it with him in Wild Hunt when he is battling ghosts and other spirits after Winter nights. By leaving the fields to him, people can do some self-reflection and contemplate their actions from the passing year, so they can make better ones in the next one.

Midsummer

This is the celebration of the longest day of the year, also known as the summer solstice. In the northern hemisphere, this falls on June 21. Although a time of festivities and joy, this holiday also has a darker side. As it is the longest day of the year, following this holiday, the days would begin to get shorter and darker, heading towards winter. Midsummer is also a time of reflection and introspection of the darker days to come. It is said that the God of light Baldur was slain during this time. Initially a great blow to the Aesir, they learned to heal and recover and move on. A timeless lesson to learn to deal with the blows of life, learn from them and move on.

Midsummer is a time to send blessings and practice to the sun and receive her life-giving light and gifts in exchange. Dagr, the God of the day, is also honored during this time. Traditionally, bonfires, speeches, songs, and dancing happen during the evening of the summer solstice.

Thorrablot

An Icelandic holiday with Viking roots, this holiday is still celebrated by some in Iceland. It is seen as a cultural celebration; however, for the heathens, this holiday is a time to celebrate Thor or the winter spirit Thorri or both.

This holiday was a sacrificial festival offered to the Gods. It was then abolished as Iceland was Christianized but brought back to life during the 19th century. On this holiday, a blot is dedicated to Thor, believed to protect humans from the Frost Giants.

A feast is laid out, and following dinner, group games are played and singing, storytelling, and drinking. The dancing then begins and usually continues until the early morning when the holiday celebrations end.

With all Asatru holidays and celebrations, there are many ways to celebrate. From prayers to a blot, this is a time to honor Thor for all of the gifts and bounties he gives to human beings.

Disting

On holiday, the beings of fertility and spring are honored. This day marks the coming spring as the harshness of winter begins to come to an end. It is also called Charming of the Plow. The plow or other tools are blessed, offerings, and then made to the Gods for a prosperous season ahead. Set times after the Plow has been blessed, a ceremonial furrow is dug and filled with cakes and other offerings.

Many celebrate and honor the Gods who bring them blessings and gifts to get them to continue to do so and show gratitude. However, Disting is in the wintertime, allowing the darker aspects to be celebrated. The God Odin is also celebrated and revered during this time.

This is a time for fertility, gratitude, and hope for impending spring weather. It is a time of gratitude to the land for looking after us and keeping us fed during the darker weather.

In modern times, we no longer rely on the soil and our tools in this way to provide us with sustenance. However, many still celebrate this holiday as a way to honor the Gods and the earth for blessings and gifts. It is also used as a time to cultivate a deeper connection with the earth. To mark the occasion, many will plant seeds or trees and give an offering to the Gods.

Ostara – March 20th–21st

The Ostara signifies the Spring Equinox and is celebrated on March 21 every year. Marking the start of the summer months, it is named after the goddess Ostara, an important Germanic deity who embodied spring and the renewal and revival of life. The name Ostara signifies the east and glory. The Ostara festival is a celebration of the revival of the Earth after months of freezing cold winters. Traditionally, homes are decorated with flowered, colored eggs, budding boughs, and branches, *etc.* The hare was the spirit animal or holy beast of the goddess Ostara. Slaying and eating rabbit meat was permitted only after taking permission from the goddess.

Holding and keeping the Ostara feast enhances the joy and happiness of the festival participants.

Walpurgis Night or May Eve

Different countries celebrate it on different days, ranging from April 30th to May 1st. In Germany, Finland, and Sweden, May Eve is celebrated on April 30th. This festival is named after a lady called Valborg or Walpurgis or Valderburger or Wealdburg. She was born in 710 in Britain and was Saint Boniface's niece. She and her brother, Wunibald, traveled to Wurttemberg, Germany, where Wunibald founded the Convent of Heidenheim. His sister, Walpurgis, became a nun in this convent. She died in 779 and was anointed as a saint on May 1st of the same year. Viking fertility festivals used to be celebrated on April 30th, and because Walpurgis was declared a saint at the same time, her name became connected with Viking fertility celebrations. Walpurgis was worshipped, similar to the way Vikings celebrated spring.

Walpurgis is one of the primary national holidays in Finland and Sweden, along with Midsummer and Yuletide. Heathens believe that Freya is the ruler of this festival because Walpurgis is the Germanic equivalent of Valentine's Day, and Freya is the goddess of love and witchcraft. In Scandinavia, the May Tree is taken out in a procession during this festival, a tradition that goes back to the fruitfulness procession of ancient Heathens. Fires are built in high places at night, and people jump over the flames for luck and good fortune.

Freyfest or Lammas or Lithasblot – July 31st–August 1st

Lammas is believed to be an Anglicized word for "hlaf-mass" or "loaves festival," a Heathen occasion of thanksgiving for bread. Heathens celebrate this festival by baking bread in the shape and figure of Freyr, followed by its symbolic sacrifice and consumption. The first of August is the time when the first fruits of harvest arrive, and in Germanic traditions, the first sheaf is offered to the Heathen gods in thanksgiving.

In today's Heathenism, Lammas (otherwise known as Lithasblot or Freyfest) is dedicated to Freyr, the fertility god, and Sif (Thor's wife), whose long golden hair is believed to symbolize the yellow fields of ripe and ready-to-harvest crops. The warriors who went to battle after the planting season returned home at this time with their battle winnings. Freyfest is the day when the hard work of harvesting and preparing for the cold winters begins.

Norse Rituals and Spells

There was no organized religion; instead, there was a spiritual practice that was deeply attached to the practice of magic. Because of their use, its symbols were sacred and bound to meaning for society as a whole. At the same time, they were also individualized by each community and each family.

Magical healers, though often revered, were also outcasts. No organization supported them in the strictest sense. So, when Christianity did come along, it was not at all uncommon to have a mix of Old Norse magic practiced side-by-side with this new religion. These practices were identified simply as the old and the new.

Old Norse magic-based faith was called "forn sidr," which means ancient custom; Christianity was referred to as the new custom or "nyr sidr." One could say that both involved sacred acts, rituals, and worship of higher powers. These were not that different from each other to the Norse people. Old Norse magic and culture were often borrowed and transformed. Ideas, including those about the importance of magic rituals, reached the Germanic tribes over time and across great stretches of land, so that traditions and incantations and stories and myths were transformed as they passed through these distances.

Norse magic is infused with this kind of heterogeneous assimilation, but it is also firmly rooted in the land and the people themselves. Some celebrations were individualized because of this. This refers to the idea of sacrifice or blót, as well as feast days and celebrations that included alcoholic drinks such as mead and food such as meat from animals who were sacrificed to the gods.

Both celebration and sacrifice often played out on specific seasons or were used to celebrate or improve fertility, ensure success in battle or a good harvest. They were also used to ensure happy births, strong marriages, peaceful burials and transitions to the afterlife. They were often customized specifically for particular communities or individuals.

Naturally, everything we know about rituals and practices from this time is also colored through the lens of the sweep of Christianity, and the belief by newly minted Christians that the rituals of the Norse people were marked by superstition or involved worshipping demons. However, much of what we're highlighting here is based on archaeological evidence, including that of the runic alphabet.

When it comes to this, some things are easy to refute, while others seem fairly easy to acknowledge and understand. In many cases, it's almost certain that private and public rituals were both taking place and likely mirrored each other. Let's start with a look at the most common and likely rituals.

Rites of Passage

Connected to birth, death, and marriage, these were also common rituals performed both in public and in private. The birth was viewed as dangerous for both mother and child, and galdr singing was often conducted in a ceremony to guide safe passage for the baby at the moment of birth.

Prayers were sent to the goddesses Freyja and Frigg. Nine nights after birth, there was also a ritual not dissimilar to a Christian christening ceremony, in which guests were invited to bring gifts and give good wishes to the child. Water was sprinkled onto the baby while being held on their father's knee. In this way, the child was formally admitted into the family. Children were also named at this time, often after ancestors or deities, or both. Setting the child on their father's knee during this ceremony officially accepted that child into society and made the parents responsible for the child's wellbeing.

Marriage

Beyond selecting one's mate, and receiving family approval for that choice, which was often made by other family members in the first place, there were many rules and rituals to be followed to summon deities to bless a marriage and avoid bad marriages. Naturally, then as now, there was no guarantee that these rituals would always prevent a bad marriage or separation. Betrothal dates were carefully set and inheritance, property, and dowry were negotiated. Once this was done, the gods were called in.

The most important ritual was the wedding itself (brudlaup). This was a public gathering of the two families involved and included a feast that lasted a minimum of three days. The goddess Var witnessed the vows. A depiction of Thor's hammer was placed on the bride's knees, asking Thor to bless her, and Freyja was always called upon to bless the marriage with fertility and luck as well. Guests would lead the bride and groom to bed. A group of witnesses would mark the consummation of the wedding and the marital relations between spouses to be legal.

The Rite of Birth

The conception and birth of a child are incredibly significant in Asatru. It is believed that once a child is conceived, the spirit of the future child is created. However, the spirit doesn't immediately enter the body of the child. Instead, it enters slowly, bit by bit, as the child grows and develops reason and intelligence (*Rite of Birth*, n.d.).

Another belief is that, before the spirit is able to submit to being incarnated, the father and mother both need to understand that the spirit of the child has existed before it is born into Midgard.

The actual birth of a child is very sacred. It is a moment that bridges the physical and spiritual worlds. Given the significance of this occasion, it is celebrated with the rite of birth.

The rite of birth is the first initiation, and it is aimed at the growth of the child's spirit self (*Rite of Birth*, n.d.).

The godhi or gydhja performs a hammer hollowing, and once done, he recites the customary words and places oil on the baby's forehead. Lastly, he does the sign of the hammer, speaks the final words, and then the ritual is complete.

The words spoken and the signs shown can differ from practitioner to practitioner and from group to group.

The Rite of Death

Many cultures and religions believe in some kind of afterlife where the spirit goes after the body has passed on. The common theory is that there's heaven, the place you go if you've lived a good life, and then alternatively, hell, where you end up if you've lived a bad life.

Theories of what happens after we die vary from person to person and from faith to faith, but to be honest, no one really knows what happens after we're gone.

According to the Asatru faith, there are two places we could end up after we pass. The first, and probably the most desirable, is Valhalla. Valhalla is a grand hall where the departed dine with the gods. Unfortunately, Valhalla and the honor of meeting the gods are reserved for those noble warriors who died gloriously in battle.

Those who died of sickness, old age, natural causes, or accidents, are set for Hel. Now, this is not the Hel you're imagining. It is simply another version of the afterlife where one is able to rest in peace with family and loved ones. Now, contrary to what you might've seen in the movies, the funeral rites don't involve flaming longboats.

In ancient times, honorable people were buried deep inside a ship that is filled with the things they might need in the afterlife. These ships were in place inside burial mounds.

An alternative practice was that of funeral pyres. It was believed that the huge pillars of smoke would aid the spirit in rising toward the afterlife.

It would be quite hard to erect funeral pyres or bury our deceased in the bellies of ships nowadays, so a few changes needed to be made.

The modern funeral rites involve burying the dead in a replica of Thor's hammer or placing it on the lid of the casket. If the deceased has been cremated, the hammer of Thor is burned.

Ancestor Worship

Another ritual was worshiping one's ancestors, which was deemed especially important because people believed that deceased ancestors could still influence or affect the life of their descendants. While they were regarded as having left the life that the living walked in, they were thought to still be living their own afterlives within Norse cosmology, depending on how they had died. When treated to the respect they deserved through proper rituals, they could bless the living and help assure their prosperity and happiness; if not, they could curse them, bring them a bad fortune, or even summon evil elves to work against them. Part of the ritual worshiping of ancestors rested on items placed within the burial mounds. These objects were considered sacred. Graves were positioned close to family homes, as ancestors were thought to protect the dwelling and its inhabitants. In a more practical sense, this also prevented the looting of graves.

Wight Worship

Land wights were spiritual beings thought to protect areas of land. As such, they were to be respected. There were many rules established so that people could avoid having any conflicts with them. They could be frightened away, which would bring bad luck. In old Norse, they were called "landvættir," or the spirits that dwell in a place or land feature. They were thought to have power and influence over the land and its wellbeing, as well as people who live or travel through it. They would either bless or curse people. Women were most often in charge of caring for land wights, placing and maintaining offerings of food and drink near locations such as wooded areas and water sources where wights were said to live. Seid, galdr, and the use of runes were all important elements of Norse rituals, used to contact deities and ancestors, for divination and omen interpretation, as well as to bless and curse.

Runes were a big part of just about any ritual, whether used for casting lots or as symbols. It is not known which particular runes were attributed to which rituals or events. The closest we can come to understanding or glimpsing rituals comes from more recent history and is based on sagas about or by Scandinavian people. In one such account, Odin required a sacrifice for a good year at the start of winter, another for rebirth in midwinter, and yet another for victory during summer.

The dead were to be cremated, ashes spread at sea or buried in the ground. The grave sites and burial mounds themselves add credence to the stories in the sagas, acknowledging them. It is only through a combination of both archeological references and written sources that we can form an idea of what rituals were used in Norse magic, both privately and publicly.

The names of specific locations or the use of symbols or runes identifying them also offer insight into these rituals. A number of locales translate to contemporary Scandinavian languages as "Thor's Temple," for example. Areas consecrated in some form of ritual were identified with the term "ve," which means the location was one of the areas where special rules applied.

There were of course specific burial sites. Images on carved jewelry or stones indicated symbols or letters in the runic alphabet that identified specific areas used in seid or other types of magic and dating back to the Iron Age.

Runes or symbols that indicated not only place markers, but also titles of magical practitioners, such as their names or positions were also found. These names indicated that these runic masters practiced in this specific location and their work was claimed and marked as such.

Written materials all indicate that there were specialists in different types of magic, confirming their position in the Old Norse society. Those who practiced seidr and galdr, as previously noted, were both revered and feared; often isolated despite having a position of great value within society.

Many of those in higher positions within Germanic societies, whether within a village, the head of a farm household, or a ruler or king, also bore the responsibility of being involved in ritual practices, either to assure prosperity, seek success in battle, or to resolve problems related to inclement weather. The leaders who refused to do so, particularly as Christianity became widespread, often found themselves losing followers, or being forbidden to preside over important seasonal occasions, including public rituals and events.

During the transition period, when Christian and magical symbols were seen frequently side-by-side, rulers and local leaders alike had to walk a fine line between preserving the old and acknowledging the new.

Spells

Spells used in Norse magic each contained a stave, a symbol that identified the runes laid out to cast that spell. Runes, as previously mentioned, were often carved on rock or wood and were viewed as a useful alphabet and a component of magic spells. The spells revealed that the runes themselves were powerful vehicles for magic.

Along with rituals, and as a part of their practice, spells were an important aspect of Norse magic, which practitioners needed to know accurately. A misinterpretation could lead to a curse instead of a blessing, losing an important battle, or poor harvests, among other things.

Even though they were prohibited by the Christian church, magic spells continued to be prominent long after Christianity came into common practice; in fact, their use became even more prominent after the Reformation, when the rituals of the Catholic Church were replaced by the far less ritualistic Protestant practices. (Mental Floss, n.d.)

In fact, despite a strict prohibition by the Lutheran Church, which became strongly enforced throughout Scandinavia, symbols became more prevalent between 1664 and 1690. This timeframe even came to be known as the new Magic Age.

But whether used predominantly in the period in which the Elder Futhark alphabet was first created or centuries later, runic invocations used to create spells were common. Exactly what these spells were used for has been lost to us because of a lack of historical records.

Modern Germanic/Norse Religion and Practices

If you think that the Norse religion is long gone, then you will be surprised to know that it still exists. You can find many groups of people around the world participating but most are concentrated within Europe and Scandinavia, where they practice a modern form of the pagan religion. They unironically call the practice Heathenry. Heathens, pertaining to those who practice Heathenry, used to be a derogatory term, and in some contexts, it still is actually. The term pertains to so-called uncivilized societies that have not been converted to Christianity. Heathenry is now a form of a new religious movement that aims to reconstruct the pre-Christian belief systems of the Norse/Germanic tribes and apply them to modern times. Practitioners of Heathenry seek to revive the ancient belief systems using whatever surviving historical source materials they can muster.

Just like the ancient Germanic religion, Heathenry has not unanimously accepted theology. Today's form of Heathenry is polytheistic, just like the ancient pagan religion. It also features a pantheon of gods and goddesses, the same ones that the early Germanic tribes used to worship. Unlike Christianity, the gods and goddesses of Heathenry are not perfect, omnipotent, and omnipresent. They think of them as having their own strengths and weaknesses. They believe that their gods will one day die like what befell Baldr in Norse mythology.

CHAPTER 5: THE NORSE RELIGION TODAY

Asatru

Asatru is a modern Icelandic term that is related specifically to the worship and veneration of the Aesir gods. Asatru is a term that is used often in formal settings among the Asatru community, more often than Norse Paganism or Heathenism. Although followers of Asatru know and believe in the Vanir gods, they don't talk about or worship any other deities but those from the Aesir tribe. Some believe that Vanatru is a direct outcome of the lack of involvement and engagement by the Asatruar with the

Vanir deities.

Asatru is a faith with multiple deities. Many of them, like Thor, have gained significance in popular culture. Asatru was systematically destroyed over hundreds of years, and its non-Christian practices were repressed. The monolithic nature of the Church demonized Pagan practices and led to the eventual downfall of Asatru. Its teachings and ideas lived on through enduring oral histories, traditions, and folklore. The faith has resurfaced in contemporary times through the Neo-Pagan movement in Europe.

Asatru has a fairly rigid and formalized set of rules to follow. The things that are expected of you as a follower of that faith could lead to a large formal community that follows the belief system. On the other hand, Heathenism and Norse Paganism seek small-scale communities that are self-sufficient in each of their traditions, cultures, and belief systems.

Although the emergence of Heathenism and Asatru are rooted in Norse Paganism, many of the modern Asatruar tend to use the term Asatru because, for the uninitiated, words like Paganism, Norse Paganism, and Heathenism tend to have a negative connotation.

One of the most important things to know about Asatru is

that there is no missionary or proselytizing events that happen. People can join the community if they want. There is nothing given in return for becoming a Heathen. You do it only if it is your calling.

Asatru is a faith largely practiced on instinct. You practice as you wish; you practice in ways that feel right to you. In Asatru, the practitioner decides how to worship and how to interact with the Gods. What makes Asatru a great faith is that it allows its practitioners this freedom.

The Asatru Association is an Icelandic religious formalized organization of Heathenry established on the First Day of Summer in 1972 by Sveinbjörn Beinteinsson, a farmer and poet. The First Day of Summer in Iceland is a national holiday and is celebrated on the first Thursday after April 18th annually. The Asatru Association was recognized and registered as a religious organization in 1973. The chief religious official or the highest office of the Asatru Association is referred to as "Allsherjargodi," an elected post.

The priests in Asatru are called Godi, and each Godi is given a congregation called godord to work with. While each godord is more or less connected to certain geographic regions, there is no compulsion to join any specific godord.

You are free to join any congregation that you like.

The legal approval allowed the organization to conduct legally binding rituals and ceremonies as well as to collect a share of the church tax, which is imposed by the tax on religious congregations to run and manage churches and their employees. Sveinbjörn Beinteinsson led this organization from its inception in 1972 until his death in 1993. During his time, the membership of this organization did not exceed 100 people, and there was not much activity. Asatru does not conform to a fixed religion, theology, or dogma. Each individual is free to have his or her own beliefs. For example, many Wiccan members are also members of the Asatru Association. The Asatru priests believe in a pantheistic perspective. The communal blot feast is the central ritual of Asatru. The priests also conduct naming ceremonies called gooar, weddings, funerals, coming of age, and other rituals too.

Core Teachings of Modern Asatru Practices

The first thing you must do when you get a calling to follow Norse Paganism is to just listen and talk to your gods. Remember that in Heathenism, gods are your friends and kinsfolk, and having conversations with them can build your rapport as well as help you to understand what you need to do and how to move ahead.

Talking to your gods is a habit you must foster early on in your journey. Modern life is so rife with professional and social activities that we forget to have conversations with our gods. However, if you persist in building this habit, like other habits such as eating healthy, exercising, etc., it can and will become part of your life routine.

You can find gods all around you in the form of spirits. You can strike up a conversation with any of them whenever you want. There is nothing to be afraid of. You can simply go out there and start speaking to Odin, Thor, or any of the gods you believe in. A vital element when speaking to gods is to remember to do so with respect. Initially, you will not know how and what each God expects from you during a conversation. Respect is a safe place to begin your conversation.

For example, if you need to speak to Odin, the king of the pantheon of Norse deities, then it makes sense to see him as a leader or father figure who can give you the powers of wisdom and clarity of thought. When you summon him, do so with humility and respect and seek his guidance and wisdom.

With another god, for example, Loki, you could have a

different approach. While respect is a given in every conversation, with gods like Loki, you can easily take an informal approach and treat him like a friend or ally. Loki is a God who will give you what you seek but will also want something in return. So, there is a sense of give-and-take camaraderie with this god.

Another critical element about having conversations with Norse gods is to have a purpose. What do you want to ask your god? Is there something bothering you? Do you seek enlightenment, clarity, or a problem to be sorted? Casual conversations like how your day at work went should be avoided because it would be wasting the time of the gods. Remember to value the time they give you when they come to talk with you. It is important to make your time with the gods meaningful.

The second step in your Asatru journey is to collect knowledge and wisdom. Do a lot of research and learn about the Asatru faith. What does it mean? What is its history? Who are gods and goddesses? Why are they the way they are? What sets them apart from human beings? What are the roles of the various gods in Asatru?

Learn about Asatru's ancestors. As you learn more about the Viking and Germanic ancestors, you will find yourself unlearning many of the elements that got incorporated into the history of the Nordic people, wittingly or unwittingly. Remind yourself that the ancestors of the Germanic tribes were highly advanced and intelligent, built fast-moving boats, and were brave warriors. They traveled long distances conquered many lands and imbibed the culture and traditions of the conquered lands. Our ancestors could have not done so much if they had simply been savages or fools.

The more you learn about Nordic ancestors and ancient tribes, the deeper your faith will become. A great way to enhance the depth of your knowledge in the domain of Norse Paganism is to try to rephrase the books, poems, and prose you are reading and studying. Also, you could check out if translating your lessons into another language will help you. Not only will this exercise build your skills in another language, but it will also help you get a deeper understanding of Norse wisdom, mythology, and ancient, forgotten knowledge.

The third step to becoming a practicing Heathen is to give offerings to the gods. The offerings you give in the form of mead, wine, meats, cheese, and other foods empower the gods, and in an empowered state, they are in a better position to help you when you need them. Again, it is time to reiterate the importance of gift exchanges in Norse Paganism.

When you give a gift or offering to the gods, they return your favor multiple times because they feel empowered by your gifts. Knowing what gifts to give to which God should be part of your research and learning process. For example, Odin is a God who only drinks and does not eat anything. So, if you offer him meat or cheese or something else to eat, he is not going to be happy, and the chances of him helping you in return are slim. Mead would be the ideal offering to Odin. You can get such important information only when you keep reading, learning, and researching the Asatru faith.

The trick is to start small. Begin offerings in little bowls, create your own hallowed verses, and seek the blessings of your gods. Don't forget to talk to them and ask them if they liked your offerings. The more you talk to them, the more you will realize that your gods are continually trying to send you messages and signs in different ways and through different people.

As you gain confidence in your ability to make offerings correctly, you can slowly and steadily enhance your offerings. There are people who started with a small bottle of mead and have ended up building firepits into which they throw steaks and meats as offerings to their gods through the fire element, but don't hesitate to take those baby steps. Start now, and sooner rather than later, you will find yourself expanding in your Asatru journey.

The fourth step in your journey is to connect with more Pagans and identify yourself with a community that you are comfortable with. Although Asatru is a sort of personal religion, it is also about ancestor worship, praying, dancing, and chanting together. It is about drinking consecrated mead together, and it is about worshipping and calling on the gods as a community. Therefore, it is important that you find your Heathen kindred and become part of it.

Also, the more you connect with other Pagans, the more you learn about your faith, and the deeper your beliefs get. Being part of a kindred is immensely useful in your research about your religion. Moreover, when other believers share their experiences with you, you will realize how similar these experiences are to your own.

It gives you a sense of identity and makes you realize and accept the presence of gods and deities all around you. You are able to counter arguments about being crazy to believe in the existence of gods. You know and accept their existence without question because you know others have had the same experiences as you.

The fifth step you should follow diligently in Norse Paganism is to have fun. Again, it makes sense to be reminded that gods and goddesses are your friends and family. You don't have to pray to them to forgive your sins and cry your heart out. You can explain your problems to them as you would to a good friend or a trusting elderly relative in your family and seek their guidance and wisdom to help you scale through the problems you face.

Unlike many mainstream religions, Asatru is not a religion where there's a set of sacred teachings that should not be analyzed or reinterpreted in any way. There is no mystery or secrets behind the teachings that only a teacher or a prophet would be able to explain to you. All the available information can be found in folklore and primary source materials, and they are freely available for anyone to read and understand according to their own knowledge and spirituality.

The Northern European gods worshipped in the Asatru religion mirror the family-focused and community-based culture of the heathens. The main deities—Odin, Frigga,

Thor, Freya, and most others are members of the same family. The commitment of the Asatru religion to their ancestors further exemplifies this close connection to the family and community they had. Ancestor worship is a large part of this religion. The two major rituals in Asatru, the Blot and the Sumble, both have a connection to ancestor worshiping.

Interacting With the Asatru Community

A great way of getting in touch with the Asatru faith and finding your way within it is by connecting to other practitioners and heathens.

Having a mentor or welcoming community can help you learn more about the faith and adds a certain nuance to some of the more abstract concepts and tenets of Asatru. It also gives you a sense of community and helps you transition to a heathenistic lifestyle.

Surrounding yourself with a supportive community also offers you companionship, which is quite important in the faith. It makes it easier to learn and grow within your faith.

The Beliefs

The Asatru faith believes that the gods and goddesses are just living beings, much like us. The only difference between them and humans is that they exist in a different realm and possess special powers. The divine beings of the Asatru faith take an active interest in the happenings of the human world and get involved in our affairs.

The Asatruars believe that divine beings can be divided into different categories. We'll be discussing the different divine beings and other mythological creatures in great detail in the upcoming chapters. In this section, we'll only be briefly looking at the different categories of creatures that the Asatruar believe in.

There are Aesirs, who are the gods worshipped by the pagans and the neopagans. The Aesir are usually characterized as benevolent, strong, valiant, and as a good force. While the Vanir are considered to be indirectly related to the Aesir clan and represent natural elements like nature and earth. Lastly, there are the Jotnar and these are giants who are always opposed to the Aesir.

The Aesir and the Jotnar are always engaged in war, and the Jotnar are symbolized as exact opposites of the Aesir. This doesn't mean there aren't any exceptions since there have been a few giants who actually cooperated with the gods, and a few giantesses have even borne the children of some Gods.

The Asatruars also believe that those who lead a righteous life and die valiantly in battle will be rewarded in the afterlife. These people are supposedly escorted by the Valkyries led by Freyja to Valhalla. The fallen warriors get to join Odin, leader of the gods, and feast on a pig called Särimner. Särimner is slaughtered, eaten, and resurrected each day. Similarly, the warriors feast in Valhalla and go out to battle daily with Odin as well.

While the brave feast in Valhalla, cowards, and immoral men go to Hifhel, which is a place meant for tormenting the wicked. However, those who are the opposite, neither valiant nor immoral end up in a place called Hel. This Hel in Norse mythology isn't akin to the hell in Abrahamic faiths. Hel is a place of perpetual calm and peace, much like limbo. Every Viking used to live by a code that dictated what they should and shouldn't do. The modern Astruars have a similar code as well and this code helps them walk a righteous path in life without deviating to any sinful ways. The Asatru beliefs are very different when compared to the other Abrahamic religions. The Asatruars worship many gods, and their religion is polytheistic; this is a belief that's much less extreme since Asatru doesn't undermine the validity of gods from other religions either. However, according to Christianity, there is a trinity composed of God, the father, Jesus, his son, and the Holy Spirit who reign supreme as one. Christians believe that there are a fixed number of realms, and all of those are ruled by one God only. The Islamic beliefs also refute the existence of any other God besides Allah, and they discard the beliefs of any other religions as well.

This is why there can be no conquests and crusades as Asatru doesn't try to impose itself on anyone. The people of North European descent can choose to follow the Asatru faith since they are direct descendants of the ones who practiced paganism before the Christians converted the majority of the world to their faith.

Asatru isn't very clear or definitive on the afterlife either. While the Abrahamic faiths believe in a place called heaven for the righteous and a burning hell for the sinners, Asatru interprets death entirely differently. The Hel that exists in Norse paganism is nothing but a place of calm and peace where the dead aren't tormented like in Hell.

However, those who commit grave sins and who are considered the lowest of the low are taken to Nastrond. It's a place of eternal punishment for the ones who lead an immoral life and don't uphold the virtues as mentioned in the "Nine Noble Virtues." The severity of a crime has to be very high to be sent to this place and only the most heinous of criminals like rapists, murderers, and oath-breakers are sentenced to suffer in Nastrond.

Heathenry

Heathenry is a new religious movement that is known by multiple other terms, including Heathenism, Germanic Neopaganism, or contemporary Germanic Paganism. It was developed in Europe in the early 20th century and is based on pre-Christian beliefs followed by the Germanic tribes from the Iron Age until the Early Middle Ages.

Heathenry is an attempt to revive and reconstruct ancient belief systems using remaining evidence from folklore, history, and archeology. Heathenry is a polytheistic belief system that focuses on a pantheon of gods, goddesses, and deities from the pre-Christian era of the Germanic regions. The followers of this new religious movement have adopted the cosmological perspectives from ancient societies and tribes. They believe in animism too, or that the cosmos, including the natural world we see around us, are filled with spirits and other divine beings and creatures.

"Heathens," as the followers of Heathenry call themselves,

believe in a system of ethics based on loyalty, personal integrity, and honor. Beliefs in the afterlife are varied but this topic does not get much attention among the Heathens. Practitioners are trying to understand and revive forgotten belief systems by using one or more of the following sources:

- Old Norse texts related to Iceland, including the *Poetic Edda* and *Prose Edda*.

- Old English recordings such as Beowulf.

- German texts of the Middle Ages such as *Nibelungenlied*.

- Archeological evidence throws light on the pre-Christian age of northern Europe.

- Folklore-based stories and tales are collectively referred to as "Lore" by Heathens.

Heathenry believers perform sacrificial rites and rituals referred to as "blots," where a variety of libations and food are offered to their deities. Most of the rituals include a ceremony called symbel, which consists of offering a toast of an alcoholic beverage to the gods. Some practitioners also perform rituals to achieve an altered state of reality through visions and wisdom from invisible spiritual beings and deities. The most popular of these rituals include the seiðr and galdr.

While some practitioners indulge in these rituals individually, some Heathens perform the ceremonies in little groups called "kindreds" or "hearths." The group rituals are usually conducted in open spaces or buildings constructed specifically for this purpose.

So, rather than wondering what it means to be a heathen, think about what you want it to mean. The faith of Asatru doesn't force a particular lifestyle or belief on its practitioners. Unlike the Abrahamic faiths, it also doesn't do any missionary work, nor is there a move to convert people to the faith.

While there aren't any prescribed practices or scriptures, there exists a few key tenets within the faith.

Heathenry predates Christianity and other Abrahamic faiths. It is believed to have been originally practiced by Northern European people who lived over a thousand years ago. These people were the Anglo-Saxon English, Scandinavians, and Germans.

While these faiths faced harsh persecution under Christian expansion, their modern-day revival has seen very little opposition. Modern heathenistic groups include Asatru and Germanic Pagan Reconstructionism.

Asatru, also known as Odinism, has thrived in Iceland and has once again become an official and nationally recognized religion in the country.

Practices of Heathenry

Heathenry celebrates two main rites called blōt and symbel (pronounced as sumble). Practitioners of Heathenry would often hold feasts based around these two main rites, like rites of passage, rites that honor a particular god or gods, and many other forms of celebration.

Originally, a blōt would include the ritual sacrifice of one or more animals to gain the favor of one or more gods or honor their ancestors. After the ritual sacrifice, a feast will be held, allowing the participants of the rite to partake of the meat of the sacrificed animal. Usually, a blōt occurs if the people wish for a particular purpose, like peace, good weather, bountiful crops, or victory.

A modern blōt no longer includes an animal sacrifice, as most people perceive it as too inhumane. It now centers upon offering food, drink, or any other items to the gods, but there will still be a feast after finishing the rite. For outdoor blōts, the items for sacrifice are often thrown into a raging bonfire. But for an indoor blōt, the participants reserve a place setting for the God or ancestor they wish to honor.

A symbel is a rite where there is a drinking horn or two filled with mead or any appropriate alcoholic beverage. After having the drinks blessed and sanctified according to Heathenistic practices, the practitioners will pass the horns around, and each will take a drink. The first round of toasts is usually offered to the gods, the second round for the ancestors, and the third is for whatever the assembled Heathens agree upon.

Besides giving offerings to the gods, most Heathens leave small gifts for the domestic "hidden folk," like the wights who live in their yards. Many Heathens have a special bowl where they place their offerings. Some even have a small altar in their garden. Often, Heathens will make a small offering for their house wight whenever they are baking bread or brewing their own mead. They do this for good luck, and to shoo away the negative energy that can spoil their produce.

You also need to be respectful towards your house wight. You have to respect their space, which you can do simply by keeping your home clean. Always do your best to be in the good graces of your hidden folk.

Morality and Ethics of Pagans

Although the name Heathen has always been associated with being uncivilized and without morals, that is the opposite of what real practitioners of the religion stand for. Heathens base their ethical and moral views on the actions of the characters in old Norse sagas. Their ethics focus mainly on the ideals of honor, hospitality, the virtue of hard work, courage, and integrity. They also strongly focus on family bonds.

The Heathen community expects members to keep their word all the time, most especially if they made a sworn oath. The main reason can be pointed to a strong individualist ethos that focuses mainly on personal responsibility. "We are our deeds" is a common motto used within the community. Most Heathenry practitioners reject the concept of sin. They believe that being guilted for your past actions is more destructive than it is useful.

The Nine Noble Virtues of Asatru

The concept of the Nine Noble Virtues is considered a modern notion, as these were codified first by the Odinic Rite in England. However, at the core, they still represent the same values as they were taught from ancient Norse sources. Moreover, these aren't just values esteemed by Old Norse people, nor are they a set of strict rules to follow. Essentially, they are guidelines for how any person should behave or what kind of choices they should make throughout their life. And most importantly, how to act when confronted with the consequences of their own actions.

1. Self-Reliance

It isn't healthy for one to wait for things to be handed to them or other people to fulfill their needs and wants on their behalf. Instead, they ought to depend on themselves, put in the time and effort, and ask for help if they need it. Asatru stresses this virtue as the religion aims for its people to grow strong and steady in their lives and the Asatru path. Through the virtue of self-reliance, the Asatruan also learns to take responsibility for their actions, predicaments, and flaws. While one might not be the cause of a problem, ultimately, it falls to the sufferer to find a solution. A self-reliant person would understand that. Rather than falling victim to the cycle of self-pity and blaming the circumstances, they would concern themselves with finding a solution. All in all, the virtue is one that, if practiced regularly, can lead to an individual making huge strides in their personal life.

2. Truth

While this should be self-explanatory, sometimes telling the truth can have undesirable consequences. Despite this, doing this can be rewarding to your mental health and your social relationships. Of course, there is a vast difference between actual truth and spiritual truth. Until you learn how to differentiate one from another, you won't be able to speak about them. Generally, the actual truth is what everyone accepts and wants to hear spoken out loud. As opposed to that, spiritual truth is what you know deep down inside you to be true. People often get stuck by only telling the first version as they want to be accepted in their social circles.

3. Self-Discipline

Gluttony had no place when it came to the Norse pagans. At a time when resources had to be conserved and where famines weren't a far-off risk, the people had to have some discipline. It was not a matter of preference but a matter of survival. In addition, to be loyal was to be self-disciplined.

It took great strength for a man to stand his ground, waiting for the enemy to approach, and great willpower for men and women to sacrifice their lives to honor the gods. Needless to say, those who had no self-discipline had no place in the tribe. Thieves and traitors were either banished, imprisoned, or killed and offered to the gods as a sacrifice. All in all, discipline was a trait favored by the gods and the people of old.

4. Honor

Contrary to popular belief, being honorable is following your own moral compass. This is why it represents the base of the value system of Norse paganism. Without honor, having all the other virtues won't mean anything, nor will they be genuine. Your honor should be the driving force you follow in every action you take and the inner voice which tells you how to differentiate right from wrong. By relying on it, your reputation will be something you can be proud of. And more importantly, you will be better able to be pleased with yourself, because the only way you can earn the respect of others is if you have developed a healthy sense of self-respect.

5. Hospitality

In looking at almost any ancient civilization, the importance of hospitality was always prevalent in forming strong connections within and without their world. This was no different in the life of Old Norse people either. For them respecting other cultures and reaching out to them was a crucial part of life. Even though they lived in groups and families isolated from one another, they opened their doors to anyone who came by. Travelers were offered shelter and protection as well. In this regard, we have to learn a lot from them. Nowadays, one rarely offers food and shelter to anyone anymore, but a few kind words could make someone's day much better.

6. Industriousness

In the same way, Norse folk didn't leave any work to the fate of gods, you should also learn the importance of working hard yourself toward your goals. You owe this to the Norse gods, your community, loved ones, and most importantly, yourself. In ancient times, actual physical labor was a necessity to put food on a table. And while in modern times you can earn a living in many other ways, you will still have to work hard to do the same. Often, it takes a lot of effort and time to reach a particular goal in life. However, if you are determined to get there, you will be able to overcome every hurdle possible. You can use almost any means to do so, but whatever you do, don't hesitate midway.

7. Perseverance

In the life of a Norse pagan, perseverance played a huge role as hardships were not uncommon. Whether it was during long and difficult sea journeys, the times when the harvest yield was not enough to feed everyone, and when defending the tribe against invaders, perseverance was the force that pushed the Northern Germanic people to innovate, develop, and improve. The same force led the gravely outnumbered Saxons to revolt against the invader King Charlemagne. Granted, this led to the Verden massacre, which reaped the lives of 4,500 Saxons, but that only emphasizes the lesson to be learned.

8. Honesty

While the God of truth, Foresti, is only mentioned twice in the Poetic Edda, honesty remains an important virtue for Norse pagans and Asatruans alike. To live life honestly, one needs to be honest in both aspects of their life, external and internal. Being truthful in the external realm doesn't just mean telling the truth when convenient. It means telling the truth regardless of the circumstances and in a professional environment, being truthful means that an Asatruan might need to stand up to a corrupt superior. In relationships, honesty means faithfulness and open communication. While external honesty is difficult, it remains much easier than internal honesty.

9. Courage

Courage in Norse myths and in ancient times came in the form of physical and mental courage in battle. War comprised a huge part of Norse myths, and it was there where acts of courage and valor were noted and valued. War was also a big part of Nordic society. Ultimately, the Northern Germanic peoples were a warrior society that was often forced to raid neighboring villages and clans to survive or forced to defend themselves against invaders. Courage was the one thing that kept warriors standing side by side, defending their homes and kin, regardless of how unfavorable the circumstances were. Death in battle was believed to be rewarded by entry to Valhalla. There, the warriors were left to feast and train in preparation for Ragnarok, where they were destined to fight side by side with Odin and the Gods.

CHAPTER 6: PRACTICES OF PAGANISM TODAY

The Blot Ritual

The communal blot festival is an important occasion in Asatru. The blot starts with hallowing the ritual with a specific formula. Another important element at the start of the blot ritual is the declaration of truce and peace among all the members present there. The chanting of verses from the *Poetic Edda* follows this ceremony. The next stage consists of passing a drinking horn wherein the participants toast and drink in honor of the gods, ancestors, and wights. Libations are also offered to the worshipped deities.

This initial part of the ritual usually happens outdoors, followed by a communal feast that usually takes place indoors. The communal feast is accompanied by entertainment in various forms, including music and dance. There are four annual blot ceremonies, including:

- The Jolablot or the Yuleblot on Winter Solstice – a special event on this day is the lighting of candles by children to celebrate the Sun's rebirth.

- The Sigurblot or the Victory blot on the First Day of Summer.

- The Sumarblot or summer blot on Summer Solstice.

- The Veturnattablot or Winter Night blot on the First Day of Winter.

In addition to these four main blots, other forms of similar rituals for individuals such as gooar and even local blots for smaller communities are conducted. All the rituals and ceremonies of the Asatru Association, including the weekly meetings, are open to the public.

Sumble

The Sumble is originally a Saxon ritual that Modern Norse Pagans have adopted. It is what usually comes after the Veizla, and it is as much a ceremony as the rest of these events. Tacitus, in particular, mentioned this ritual in "Germania" with a remark about how amazing it was that the tribesmen would just air their personal matters before everyone in their community. Sumble is also mentioned in several other literary works such as Heimskringla, Beowulf, and the Jómsvíkinga saga.

Tradition holds that any boast, oath, or toast uttered during a Sumble will go straight into the Well of Wyrd and will be heard by the gods. Words spoken during a Sumble must be taken seriously at all times since each participant affects the Wyrd for ill or for good.

Sumbles were always performed in a closed hall to ensure that the event would remain sacred and separated by everyday life and that it was taking place outside space and time. That way, participants would feel a connection to gods and ancestors, as well as the spirit world.

Three positions occur in a Sumble apart from being a simple participant. Those are the Drighten, Thule, and Valkyrie.

The Drighten is the one who is in charge of the Sumble. They declare the beginning of the Sumble, as well as the beginnings and endings of rounds.

The Thule is the one who guards the luck of the kindred and the hall. The Thule's task is to challenge any oath or boast that might poorly affect the luck of the kindred or might potentially be offensive to the gods. If a Sumble participant is challenged, they get the chance to re-affirm their oath or boast and are allowed to call upon someone present in support so that they can speak for them. However, no one should be offended if they're challenged as the Thule's only concern is to safeguard the örlög (destiny) and luck of the group.

If the challenged one doesn't complete his oath or his boast is false, then by challenging him, the Thule notes that the group has notified the Gods, so the sole blame falls on the challenged and not on the group.

The Valkyrie should be a woman. However, it doesn't matter if one isn't available. She is the one who blesses the drink and is the one who must at least pour the first horn-full of drink. That is because women were believed to have magical properties of nourishing and healing

Sumbles are usually dedicated in distinct ways, depending on the content of the rounds. Usually, the first one is for the gods and the spirits, the second round is for the heroes and the ancestors, and the third is most commonly an open round for the oaths, boasts, and toasts. There might be more rounds after the third, which usually involve feats of song, poetry, etc.

At the end of each round, the remainder of the drink is poured in a hlautbolli. Some are collected in a ladle from the bowl and poured back into the drinking horn, the horn is refilled with more blessed drink, and the rounds continue.

This way, the gods, the ancestors, and the mortals share drinks.

No matter the number of rounds, it is important to remember these things:

- A Sumble is a sacred ritual, and the atmosphere should be preserved as such and not devolve into a simple party.

- It is considered improper not to give one's full attention to whoever is holding the drinking horn during a Sumble.

- Interruptions, commentary, and starting irrelevant conversations or shouting are considered very rude.

- Getting drunk at Sumble is also considered quite rude.

- Participants should pay attention to all toasts and say "Hail" when one drinks.

- If a participant can't communally drink from the horn for any reason, then they may kiss the side of the horn. No one will consider it odd or strange in any way.

The Bragarfull is the Scandinavian equivalent, meaning "promise-cup," "chieftain's cup," or "best cup" used to be a ritual where people would drink from a cup or a drinking horn during ceremonies and would swear oaths while the cup was imbibed by a chieftain or was being passed around to those assembled.

Profession

This is one of the most important ceremonies in Asatru. This is a profession of one's belief in the Gods and is considered an important turning point in an individual's life. It is seen as the beginning of a full new understanding and perspective of the self. Despite the sacredness and magnitude of it, it is a rather simple and short ceremony. This usually occurs during a regular meeting or before or after the blot.

The idea behind this is to commit Asatru. It should only ever be taken from a place of true faith, following deep thought and prayer. Following a profession, one has left behind any other faith. Any identity tied to any other faith system has been destroyed. If this isn't entirely comfortable for some people, it is recommended to leave the profession until one feels completely ready to commit themselves to the Gods. There is never any pressure applied to get one to profess; it is entirely within their remit. Coerced or false professions cheapen the deep and undying commitment of the community and the faith. The rituals of Asatru are open to all whether or not a profession has been undertaken. Following a profession, a Sumbel of nine rounds is usually held. Each of these rounds is dedicated to one of the values Asatru.

Talisman

A runic talisman, also known as an amulet, is an object or charm that is inscribed with a rune that the user can carry with them. Depending on the rune or runes that you use, your talisman can bring you good fortune, safe travels, prosperity, or ward off evil and misfortune.

You can wear your talismans like a necklace or ring, clip them to your bag like a keychain, place them on your altar or somewhere close by, carry them with you in your pocket or wallet, or give it as a gift. How you choose to create your talisman is based on its purpose and your intentions.

Creating a Talisman

When preparing your space and creating your talisman, there are different ways it can be done. Much of this depends on your beliefs and worship. For example, someone who follows the path of Odinism might choose to make their talisman on a Wednesday, the sacred day of Odin. Some people chant oaths or passages that are sacred to them, while others choose to create their talisman in a sacred space, surrounded by crystals or Epsom salt.

Timing is also something to consider. If you're looking to increase and attract magic, you should create your talisman during a waxing moon. In contrast, creating it during a waning moon is better for banishing negative energy or evil. The steps below are the basic instructions for creating a talisman. Any additional choice of sacred bonding is based solely on your beliefs:

- The first thing to do when creating a talisman is to gather the material you want to inscribe. This can be wood, stone, paper, parchment, bone, antler, leather, clay, or even seashells. You can choose whatever material you want to use, though organic materials are recommended because those materials come directly from the Earth. This enhances the magical energy as it's organic.

- If you choose to use wood, you might find that using softwood, like pine or fir, works better than hardwood, like maple or birch. It's less likely to crack and split when you're carving or burning it. Also, consider how you're obtaining that wood. Some believe that harming any living plant is considered taboo and claim that using a piece of dead branch is just as effective. Others believe that asking for permission and acknowledging the sacrifice made by the tree is part of the ritual. Whichever way you choose to obtain your wood is based on your own beliefs, as long as you aren't recklessly cutting down living organisms carelessly for your own benefit.

- When you have your material chosen, think of why you're creating a talisman. What purpose do you want it to serve? Is it a keychain you'll clip on your luggage or backpack? You might want to use the rune Raidho for movement and safe travels. Perhaps you've thought of making a charm to cheer up your sick friend? Using the rune Uruz for health and strength can help them to heal.

- Knowing why you're creating a talisman helps you determine which runes would be best to use. Then, draw the runes on paper before inscribing your talisman. You don't want to ruin your talisman because you didn't take the time to create a rough sketch of your runes first. This especially applies if you're using more than one rune because you'll be making a bindrune, which is a design that combines more than one rune into a single design. The design is wholly your creation. There will be more information about this in the Bind Runes section.

- You might also choose to make a bindrune of your name. If you do this, make sure to use your true name. This doesn't have to be your given name, your full name, or your initials. You want to use the name that you feel most comfortable with. If it's a nickname or a name you use within your pagan path, that's fine. As long as it's the name that you feel most truly captures your sense of self, you should use it. This makes your talisman personal to you. If you're making it for someone else, you'll create a bindrune using their name. You'll translate these letters using the runic alphabet and practice writing it on paper before inscribing your talisman. It's suggested that you destroy your practice rune after you're finished with it and never leave it lying around. Whether this is myth or truth is up to you.

- After you've got your design figured out, you're ready to make it permanent. The material you're using will determine how you inscribe your talisman. If you're using wood, you might choose to carve, burn, or paint the wood. However, burning won't work if you're using paper or parchment.

- You can use a wood-burning kit, dremel or rotary tool, knife, paintbrush, pen or marker, or anything else that you have lying around that would work with your material.

- While you're inscribing your talisman, concentrate on the powers of the runes you chose. This should be a ceremonious occasion, so feel free to burn incense, play music, chant, or anything else that connects you spiritually. Old Norse beliefs include animism, which means that all parts of the natural world have spirits. This includes rivers, mountains, grass, trees, and anything else that can be found in nature. Let the spirits of the wood or the stone know that you're grateful for its existence and for allowing you to use it.

- The ancients believed that your rune needed to be marked red to symbolize blood and sacrifice. Blood is believed to fuel the spiritual forces within the rune. Some people choose to use their blood to dye their rune. If you choose this route, make sure that the rune is only for you and not to be given to someone else. Your blood on the talisman makes it personal to you. If you choose to use paint as a form of dye, you might consider using a shade of red, green, or blue. These colors are more attuned to the natural world, though you can use other colors if you choose. It depends on how closely you follow the ancient ways.

- Once it's dried, you can coat your talisman with shellac, or other clear coatings. You can adorn your talisman with other natural elements like crystals or feathers. If you're making a necklace, you can add a chain or a cord.

- Your talisman is finished. Now, you need to charge it or activate it with magic. Similar to when you were inscribing the talisman, you can chant the name of the runes, summon your deities or the spiritual energy of the runes, burn incense or candles, use the energy from crystals, or anything else that connects you spiritually to magic. Hold the talisman in your hands and concentrate on the desired power and energies you're bringing to the object.

- Bundle the talisman in a cloth and wrap a cord around it nine times. Then, you'll leave your wrapped talisman in the darkness to charge, which symbolizes growing in the womb and the birthing of your talisman. The time period you leave it should be in increments of nine; nine minutes, nine hours, nine days, *etc.* You can also leave it under a full moon or a crystal grid to charge.

- After the talisman has served its purpose or you're finished using it, you should burn it or bury it to release the magic.

Altar

Not everyone has an altar, but many heathens have some kind of setup at home where they can focus their attention when they talk to the gods. An altar is made up of many different things that are meaningful to the person who made it. Do not think of an altar as something that *must* contain certain things—it can contain exactly the things you want and nothing else. An altar is a space that you build or create for yourself, composed of only the things that make you feel comfortable. I have seen heathens use two kinds of altars: indoor altars and outdoor altars.

Indoor Altars

With an indoor altar, you obviously have more options for putting things on it. If, for instance, you are a person who feels closely attached to things such as heirlooms and you want to put them on your altar, they will be more secure on your indoor altar than an outdoor one. You also have the option to put things on your indoor altar that would otherwise perish outdoors or be taken by animals.

Creating your indoor altar is rooted in how you intend to commune with the spirits. For instance, if runic meditation is something you like to do, it will be meaningful to place your set of runes on the altar. You can also place a picture, drawing, or painting of your favorite God or pictures of multiple gods. You can put rocks and plants there, too. If you like to interact with the gods and spirits through drink and food, you can have items on your altar for that. Drinking horns are very popular among Ásatrúar, especially ornately carved cow horns. You may also consider having a plate on which you put things as offerings to the gods and spirits.

Many indoor altars are focused on ancestors rather than on gods and spirits. People place pictures of their family and deceased ancestors on the altar. They hang items that used to belong to their loved ones on the altar, and in that way, the altar becomes a space in the home where you can communicate with your long-gone ancestors. Most heathens believe that the dead do not die. They live on in our memories, in our hearts, and our surroundings. That idea is more important than any "paradise" or death-realm beyond our living world, because it means that our ancestors never abandon us.

In my house, we have a family altar, which combines the ancestors and important spirits of our combined families. We have important items on our altar, including pictures, which have belonged to our grandparents and great-grandparents. Aside from that, we have flowers and wooden carvings, ritual instruments that we use in ceremonies, gifts and offerings for the gods and spirits, and many more items. All in all, what you put on your altar comes down to how you want to communicate with the gods, spirits, and ancestors.

Outdoor Altars

An outdoor altar is naturally different from an indoor one. Of course, not everyone lives somewhere that will allow for an outdoor altar, but those who do may opt for an outdoor altar. The benefit of an outdoor altar is that you can pour libations to the gods and spirits directly onto the ground. You can fashion a full space that is only to be used for ritual acts, and you can make it as beautiful as you want—for instance, as a part of your garden.

Some heathens who have the space for outdoor altars design a part of their property as a little grove with trees and sometimes a pond. Others have a large rock that they put things on for the gods and spirits. Others have an altar built of several larger and smaller rocks. Some like to mark off the area around their altar with a circle. Often, the circle is comprised of smaller rocks, wooden sticks, small fences, or ropes.

While the ancient stories do not describe indoor altars, some give indications of how sacred outdoor spaces were created. In the Icelandic sagas, they talk about the type of sacred site called a **vé**. The vé is a sacred space that is marked off with **vébönd**, bonds, or chains that are attached to hazelnut sticks. In several stories, there are also descriptions of special rocks and boulders, as well as ponds, lakes, and creeks, which were used as focus points for personal rituals.

CHAPTER 7: RUNES YESTERDAY AND TODAY

History of Runes

The word '*Rune*' comes originally from the Old English word '*rún*' meaning a secret or a mystery. It is also related to the Old High German word known as '*runa*' which conveys the meaning of a secret conversation, or a whisper. At last, the word rune is also found in Old Norse as '*rúnir*' or '*rúnar*' which carries the meaning of magical signs and hidden lore.

The earliest examples of rune usage are found among the Germanic people who used the runes from at least the 2nd century B.C. into the middle ages. However, as our preliminary linguistic studies have pointed out, the word is found in many geographical areas conveying similar meanings. It would not be hard for us to assume that the concept of the rune is very old and does not necessarily correspond with the physical artifacts left with us from past history. The concept of a rune goes far back into the Indo-European family tree and existed among the ancestors of our ancestors.

Currently, over 6000 runic inscriptions have been found altogether. The highest concentrations of these are located in the Northern European landscape. This fact alone can help us dispel the myth that runes originated from the Mediterranean script, a theory that should altogether be disposed of permanently by practitioners of the Asatru faith. If this theory was true, we could expect to find the highest concentration close to the Mediterranean civilizations in the South.

The term Futhark comes from the first 6 letters of the Runic alphabet, making it easy for us to coin a name. These runes are: F (Fehu), U (Uruz), Th (Thurisaz), A (Ansuz), R (Raidho), and K (Kenaz). More about this will be written later. One must also be aware that runes existed for the different people of the North. Today we have the vestiges of an Anglo-Saxon Runic System, an Old Norse Runic System, and an Icelandic Runic System. While similar to each other, they do have their differences.

For a variety of reasons, the meaning of the runes of the Elder Futhark was lost over time. The Futhark was re-discovered in 1865 by Sophus Bugge a Norwegian philologist and linguist.

The Runes were originally created with twenty-four in number, being arranged in three rows of eight Runes. The pattern of the arrangement was itself carefully contrived. Later in time, Norway and Denmark shortened this pattern to compose a system of only sixteen Runes. The English Saxons lengthened it in some places to thirty-three Runes. Despite these changes, Master of the Runes worked with the original twenty-four Runes. They may have used later pictographs, but the Runic potencies remained the same. Any attempts to change the Futhark orders are doomed to mislead, for the ancient order is magickally precise.

The twenty-four Rune Futhark is ordered in three rows of eight Runes. Each row is known as an Aett or Airt.

- Know how to cut them, know how to read them,

- Know how to stain them, know how to prove them,

- Know how to evoke them, know how to score them,

- Know how to send them, know how to spend them.

For our purposes, we will see the Elder Futhark as a set of traditional codes or magic characters (galdr) through which information can circulate between the material and immaterial worlds.

The true secret of the runes is learning the meta-knowledge underlying their arrangement. This knowledge is omnipresent in the runic system. For example, Jera is the Y-rune and means "year." This rune also carries with it the 12th position in the Elder Futhark. Coincidence or not? It is this knowledge that has been lost in the sands of time, and it is this knowledge that Asatru aims to reclaim. For a complete guide to the runes read the book "Master of the Runes."

The origin of Runes can be traced back to the Germanic people of the 1st and 2nd century AD, a period which has a lot of similarities with the Common Germanic era linguistically, and were later modified to make it possible for them to be used in many other languages like Danish, English, Frisian, Gothic, Norwegian, Hebrew, Icelandic, Lithuanian, German and Russian among Semitic languages which were as a result of trade interactions with the traders from Silk Road known by Khazars.

Runes can be read from right to left or from left to right and this is what contributes to making the translation of the characters quite a challenge, but some historical inscriptions which were translated by the masters of the time have been discovered and they have helped to a big extent to attach meaning to Runes.

Runes are also known as Elder Futhark - this is the Nordic runic alphabet, consisting of 24 runes. The runes themselves are symbols, written or carved on stone or wood, or even paper. They are believed to be a gift from Odin, the Nordic god, and it has the magical power to attract love, money, friendship, and success. The word "rune" itself means "secret" or "whisper," and this makes the runes magical symbols very mysterious for that same day. From a scientific point of view, it is difficult to learn the age of runes. Some researchers tend to believe that they have existed for more than 3 thousand years. Most scientists agree that they are not more than 2 thousand years old.

From the mythological point of view, the runes are the gift of Odin, who was hung on the tree of life for nine days and nights and was blessed with the wisdom of the runes. Later, he passed on his knowledge to humans.

Runes were used mainly as a magic Alphabet. They were used for divination and prediction of the future. They were also used to sculpt whole sentences called "runic formulas or runic scripts." Such formulas were aimed at attracting wealth and success by magical means. Runes have also been used to make talismans and amulets called "bindrunes." A bindrune is a symbol made of two or three different runes connected to each other, and it is a very powerful magic talisman.

In the old days, runes were used by northerners, Vikings, and inhabitants of the British Isles. Northern Europe was also not without runes. They were used by druids for magical rituals, winning victory in battle, attracting a good harvest, *etc.* still today runes are used. However, no one writes more about it. The Elder Futhark symbols are still used for divination and the creation of talismans. You can find many books on the topic, and even the Guild of modern Druids who still use runes. You can also learn runic magic for your own purpose; if you want, there are many resources out there.

With runes, you can attract good work, love, and friendship, business success, material and spiritual wealth, health, and many other things. If you're looking for a peaceful but mysterious magic system, the runes will be the best to start with.

Uses

Runes first started out as a form of writing and, to this day, still have a strong set of roots in the world in terms of communication. Since you are reading this now, it is very likely that you are already familiar with at least the concept of runes. Don't worry, you are not alone: As we have mentioned in previous chapters, runes, rune writing, and the runic language Havre both fascinated and captured the imaginations of people since their original inception thousands of years ago. Runes were at first considered a secret language known only to the wisest and most esoteric of individuals, such as shamans, wandering sages, or particularly celebrated god-kings the likes of Odin the All-Father, patron God of Nordic mythology.

Ancient cultures over the centuries of human civilization have used runes to empower amulets, jewelry, and weapons borne by warriors into battle, which in turn were believed to bestow magical powers of protection or other enchantments on those who wore them. Some warriors, such as the legendary berserkers, are believed to have tattooed runes all over their body, believing that the signs would grant them great strength and make them invulnerable to sword cuts and arrow strikes. Runes have been carved on graves and massive standing stones, both to commemorate a great person or celebrate an achievement, as well as to help guide the spirit to the afterlife. Runes have been spoken and sung as part of magical incantations, and of course, cast in the form of runestones believed to hold the power to divine the future. In fact, even the Nazis that rose to power in Germany in the years leading up to World War II were purportedly fascinated by runes and the supernatural powers that one could glean from knowing their meanings.

Even in the modern-day, we see renditions of runes in popular culture, especially in fantasy novels and movies such as **Lord of the Rings** and the **Harry Potter** series, and even in video games like **The Elder Scrolls: Skyrim**. One interesting observation one could make about all these instances is that runes are almost always associated with some sort of mystical significance. Even in the stories and fantasy fiction, we tell today, we like to attribute at least a small degree of underlying magical power to these cryptic symbols from civilization's storied past. Whether they contain actual magic, are used as symbols and charms, or contain the power to foretell the future or tap into the distant past, runes have never failed to captivate the minds of their readers.

Unfortunately, one obvious downside to this enduring popularity is that a great deal of confusion and misinformation, honest or deliberate, has cropped up about runes. As a result of this sad happenstance, a lot of popular assumptions about the nature, the significance, and possible uses of runes, have been rendered inaccurate, distorted by time and historical events. As well, the meaning behind some symbols—for example, the infamous swastika—is now almost universally and instinctively perceived as a sign representing absolute evil and human cruelty, which is a far cry from its original meaning.

In Germanic runology, various runes represented a certain letter in the alphabet, and these also were used in representing whole words. 'Whole words' are mentioned here because an important tool in understanding how runes are perceived lies in language itself. As our understanding of language has evolved, so has our understanding of runes.

Runes can also be used in another way of helping to communicate with those that have passed on. While this is a very difficult and controversial thing to do, some will generally say that you need to be careful when doing this, as it is not something that you need to try and do on your own. You need to make sure that you talk to a rune caster before you try this type of procedure as this can lead to some issues or, in most cases, will not lead to anything at all if you are not experienced enough in the use of runes. I heard of a person that tried this one time and did not have the best of experiences when doing this. They had heard that runes might be useable in talking with a loved one that had recently passed. They even went to a rune caster and they were not able to make the connections to the loved one that had died. This is usually the result of these types of inquiries.

In closing, runes have a load of power that they can offer a person in terms of learning a new language, having a better understanding of aspects of their life, or, in rare cases, being able to communicate with a loved one that you never got to say goodbye to. In all, runes will make an impact in your life and are very much something that you will want to make sure that you learn all that you can about to get a better understanding of.

Runic Alphabet

Each rune cast has a specific meaning behind it as described below. (Gronitz, n.d.) Today, some users also attribute a color to each rune; however, in traditional Norse magic, this was not the case.

Fehu

Fehu sounds like the letter "f," and it represents cattle, which was at the time an indication of wealth. But when cast for divination its purpose is power, control, new beginnings, and wealth that is moveable. This can be money or credit, rather than something held in place, like land. This rune provides the power needed to "obtain wealth as well as the power to hold on to it." (Gronitz, n.d.)

Uruz

Uruz sounds like a double "o," "oo." It represents a wild ox. It's a rune of power, like Fehu, but its power cannot be owned or controlled. When cast, it signifies that a personal success may be close at hand; it was used in charms and talismans for healing.

Thurisaz

Representing the sound "th," and a thorn, Thurisaz when cast reveals an ability to passively resist conflict. A protection rune can foretell a change that could come without warning. It can also be used as a defense, protecting against adversaries of all kinds.

Ansuz

Ansuz sounds like "aah." It represents the mouth or a divine breath, and when cast, it represents stability and order. This rune identifies the intellectual and the divine breath of all creation.

Raidho

Representing the letter "r," Raidho translates as wheel or riding. When cast, its meaning is a focus of energy at the right place and time to obtain desired goals. It indicates motion or change.

Kenaz   <

Kenaz, or "k," represents a torch. When it is cast, it's seen as a rune about learning, understanding, knowledge and teaching, something that can allow greater clarity.

Gebo   X

Representing the letter "g" and with a literal meaning of the gift, when it is cast, Gebo stands for connection, honor, an exchange of gifts, a blessing, and the honor that the gods grant for a person to have life itself.

Wunjo   P

Representing the sound for both "w" and "v," Wunjo stands for joy. When it is cast, it reveals the balance in even the most chaotic world, as well as fellowship, common goals, and well-being. It also reveals the idea of good news in the future. If this rune should appear in a reading, the expectation is that good news will come to you.

Hagalaz   H

Hagalaz signifies the sound of the letter "h." It represents hail or hailstones, and when cast refers to constricted situations that will eventually flow smoothly, just as a hailstone will melt and wash away. While it can signify challenges or adversity, it also signifies the ability to overcome them.

Naudhiz

Representing the sound for the letter "n" and the idea of need or necessity, Naudhiz, when cast, can be read as revealing a restriction of possibilities due to our own wants and our own power to break free.

Isa

The sound of Isa represents a double "ee"; as a word, the symbol stands for ice; when cast, it is often thought to represent a suggestion to stop an activity until change comes; but like a melting icicle, it too can be freed.

Jera

Jera forms the "j" sound and represents a harvest, year, or season. When it is cast, it indicates a life cycle and the importance of going with nature's flow and not against it in order to obtain one's desired goals.

Eihwaz

Eihwaz sounds like "eo" or "æ" and represents the yew tree. Its cast meaning is that of a magical protector and helper, and it is said to reveal the idea that with every ending comes a new beginning.

Perdhro

Perdho sounds like "p" and represents, among other things, the cup used to contain dice. When cast, it stands for the uncertainties of life and free will. It serves as both a rune of memory and one that is involved in problem-solving.

Elhaz

A double "zz" sound, Elhaz represents the elk. When cast it signifies protection, power, and ideas of defense. It is often used to protect both people and property.

Sowulo

Forming the "s" sound, Sowulo stands for the sun, and its meaning when cast refers to the light in the darkness and the ability to see things more clearly.

Teiwaz 

Representing the sound of "t," Teiwaz is the creator; when cast, it promises us success without personal sacrifice, including in legal areas if we are in the right.

Berkana

Just like the symbol appears to us in English, this Norse rune has the sound of the letter "b." It stands for the birch tree or twig. It represents a new beginning and is also a power-filled birth rune when it is cast.

Ehwaz

Ehwaz sounds like "eh," and in the literal alphabet, stands for the word horse. When it is cast, this rune expresses the idea that there needs to be a natural flow for success. It gives one power and the use of good intentions to achieve success.

Mannaz

Mannaz sounds like the letter "m" and represents man or

human. It has many different powers when cast. Its casting may reveal that we can achieve our full potential in life, remind us that we have shared experiences with other human beings, and allow us to achieve the upper hand in disagreements and disputes.

Laguz

Laguz sounds like "l" and represents water or a lake. When cast, the power and flow of water are represented, revealing the need to flow ourselves, in order to fully achieve our powers and abilities.

Inguz

Inguz is an "ng" sound and literally represents the idea of fertility. The rune's cast meaning is about spreading our energy widely. It also reveals the protection of our homes, as well as the idea that we must use gained wisdom in order to increase our power over time and then release it at once as needed.

Dagaz

Dagaz sounds like the letter "d" and means day. Its cast

meaning is about opposites and their stability, a kind of yin/yang dynamic as it were, such as that between light and dark or day and night. It prevents harmful energy from reaching you, but allows good energy to come through.

Othala 

Sounding like a long "o," Othala means home or an ancestral, sacred land and is a rune that represents wealth, like Fehu. However, Othala's wealth can't be sold and instead represents the wealth of friends, family, and heritage. It also reveals a state of present existence and maintaining it. (Gronitz, n.d.)

CHAPTER 8: THE FOUNDATIONS OF DIVINATION

Runes In Divination

Magic is often a label that is stuck on the Norse, the Vikings, and pagans in general, but the word 'pagan' really only means "someone who doesn't believe in the most popular god or gods of the time." This is a simplistic breakdown of it, but when you boil it down this is what it means. Maybe this is why it scares people, but the general populace has always been afraid of what they can't or don't want to understand.

Anything strange or 'supernatural' will always be viewed as magic, and the ones who shout the loudest that it doesn't exist would be the first to just label that very phenomenon as science if it was suddenly proven. This is why we must always keep an open mind when we think about magic as a whole, as if you genuinely believe in it, then the first, and most important, step has been made.

Oftentimes, when people think of the Vikings and their many gods, they conjure images of human sacrifices and suffering, but the gods that these people worshipped were seen as forgiving, helpful entities who cared and loved for their people. It wasn't all blood and death as the movies would have us believe, and the magic and divination that they practiced were always based on doing good, such as protection for their families or sending the fallen to a better life.

Odin, they believed, committed an act of unimaginable bravery and selflessness to become their most revered and loved of all gods when he gave himself up as a human sacrifice by hanging himself on a tree for three days. When he did this, he was given the knowledge of the Viking Runes, which gave him the most powerful magic known to man.

These runes held all of the power in the universe, and Odin brought the knowledge of them back to Earth to share it with his people. Because of this, it is easy to understand just why the Norse put so much faith in them. Along with their importance in their societal and intellectual growth, the force of strong emotions that they brought out in the people that used them is there for all to see when we look at conquests of the Viking Age and the growth of the Norse people in general.

Much like the advertising we mentioned, or the hypnosis,

we cannot even begin to think of the effect that these runes had on the people who truly believed in them. Most of the reason that the modern-day naysayers dismiss them so easily is that they do not believe. As we have mentioned earlier in this chapter, the power of the mind is astronomically immense, and when we harness it onto something as powerful as runes and divination, then the possibilities are endless.

Too often, we are held back from wondrous things by a fear of what others will think or how they will react, but if you really open your mind to anything, then what will happen will always be magical, in whatever way you view it. We cannot ever be told what to believe in. This is what carried our forefathers through darker times when magic and spells were what brightened their world.

Another thing that is important to understand is that the rune-masters of old would have been one of the few, or maybe even the only, people in the village that would be what we would consider literate. This is because education and things such as this were seen as secondary whereas physical strength and battle scars were viewed as the essentials. Regardless of this, when a rune-master would read and write the runic script, it would have blown people's minds, which is why we have to always try and slip our mindset back to these times when we consider a lot of what we are discussing.

Inevitably, when these rune-masters would regale their people with perfectly remembered tales of the gods, or explain in detail each rune and the powers they possessed, it was, of course, a form of magic, as only a select few could do it. To the vast majority, what they were seeing and hearing was not possible for their minds to even begin to comprehend. If they lived now, they would believe it to be camera tricks.

Runes were carved or painted on many materials. This was always to bring luck, protection, and safety to their families. When a warrior came back from battle unhurt and discovered that his family was also safe then his charm worked. The magic was there right in front of them.

The use of runes in divination is one of the key aspects of Norse magic. This use is bound together with the runic alphabet itself and Norse history. With that in mind, we've examined the known origins of this magic, and the major role that runes have in galdr, one of the two main forms of magic in Early Scandinavia. Galdr specifically uses the symbols of the runic alphabet for divination. We've also looked at the runic alphabet in terms of literal meaning, sound, and magical interpretation when cast for divination. So, let's take a look at some of the ways in which you can cast runes and perform a rune reading.

The ancient Norse symbols inscribed on runes allow us, just as the rune masters learned long ago, to use our intuition and inner wisdom to utilize them for divination purposes.

Divination includes not just the runes themselves, but types of rune layouts, from a single rune to a three-rune cast, as well as casts in either multiple of three or in odd numbers. You will find rune layouts including all of the forms used, as well as an insightful 24-rune casting often performed at the beginning of a new year, whether on a person's birthday, or New Year's Day. This extensive casting focuses on the entire year.

Rune layouts aside, you'll find there are three primary ways to cast runes. First, they can be cast randomly by throwing them, whether on the ground or onto a piece of fabric. Second, you can choose to read only the runes tossed down that land in the upright position and not to read those in the reversed position, or read the reversed runes as well, which have a different interpretation. Third, you can also keep your runes within a pouch or bag in your least dominant hand, consider the question or situation in which you are seeking guidance, and pull-out runes individually, positioning them in whatever layout pattern you choose. (Talisa and Sam, n.d.) Rune stones can be purchased pre-made, or you can inscribe your own on wood, stone, or even crystals, just as was done in early Norse times. If making your own, be sure to use 24 similarly sized small objects. Runes can also be etched into good luck charms or carved into candles as your own personal talismans.

Reiterating the history of the runic alphabet, runes were used in a common, traditional sense just like we use our alphabet today. They were also used for divination. Well-practiced rune masters were used to cast runes for the purpose of magic. These rune masters cast and read the runes after throwing them onto a cloth or directly on the ground, usually with their eyes turned up to the sky to get guidance from the Norse gods. Looking up was one way to be sure they would not influence the casting in any way through personal feelings or prejudices. These masters would not read any upturned runes; when first used, runes were not read in reverse.

A more modern way to cast runes usually involves pulling each stone individually from a pouch, following an intuitive and selective impulse to choose each rune stone and lay it out, forming a spread of runes in whatever fashion or pattern you choose. (Talisa and Sam, n.d.)

The practice and use of runes is the most common form of magic within the Asatru faith. But, what are runes? And what value do they bring to the faith?

Well, in simple terms, runes are alphabetic symbols that form the language of the cosmos and that allows us to interpret cosmic messages. As I've mentioned with seidhr, if you are interested in working with runes, I really suggest you do additional reading and research. The journey toward reading and being able to interpret runes isn't easy and often leads to a deep transformation of the self.

You need to approach all forms of magic with respect, reverence, and a fair bit of caution. Runes can affect our lives and are not something to be handled lightly.

In the modern Asatru faith, runes are mainly used for divination. Runes are particularly valuable as a tool for divination because they allow the practitioner to commune with the deep subconsciousness of their souls. Runic practice can aid in building inner strength and trust.

At this point, I think it's important to clarify the kind of divination runes can aid with. Runic divination will not give you the numbers to the lotto. Instead, it will tell you where you've been and where you're going. In some cases, it might even reveal a path that you might've been looking for.

This interpretation of divination stems from the belief that the forces of our fate can, to a certain extent, be examined and interpreted in order to tell us our future. Given that our future is determined by our actions, if we change our actions in response to a known future, we can change that future.

A common method to read and interpret runes is by pulling out three runes, each representing the past, present, and future. By looking at these three aspects, and especially the ways they relate to each other, it is believed that you will be able to read the future, within reason, of course.

Modern Asatru runic practices make use of the 'Elder Futhark,' which is a runic alphabet. There are generally 24 runes that are used.

In addition to divination, runes can also be used in active magic, but this practice is less common. One method of practicing active rune magic is to carve what is known as a 'bind rune.' A bind rune is often made up of more than one symbol, which, when combined, produces some desired outcome.

Another method of active runic magic is the galdr or chant magic. However, for the purposes of this chapter, I'll be focusing specifically on runic divination as it is the most common form of magic practiced within the Asatru faith.

I do suggest you do more research on the matter before diving in.

That being said, this section discusses how to cast runes for divination and the interpretation of runes.

Choosing Your Runes

There are many online sites or specialty stores that sell runes of all kinds. Materials that they are carved in the range from stone and wood to amethyst and crystal. The choice is completely yours, and I am certain that once you hold the one that suits you best in your hand, you will know instantly which one is for you.

If you decide to make them yourself, then be sure to craft them in even sizes. Once you have chosen your material, it is vitally important to make sure that they are flat on one side. The last thing you want is for one or two of the runes to be unreadable when you cast them. This will only lead to doubt and confusion as to what the casting meant and how to proceed.

Storing your runes safely is important and it is common practice to do so in a draw-string pouch. Oftentimes, if you purchase them online or in a store, they will come with such an accessory. If you craft them yourself, then a separate pouch or even a small box works just as well. Just remember to always keep them safe and easy to find.

If you are buying a new set of runes, be sure that they are of the Elder Futhark and not one of the variations that followed. These versions *do* work, but we have been discussing the benefits of the Elder here, so it would simply be confusing to go another way. Also, try to make sure that you don't go cheap. Although some people will see them as just pieces of rock or wood, the cheaper versions will be uneven and the symbols will fade over time.

Of course, if you make them yourself there will always be a danger of this, but the difference is that you will be able to touch them up without any issues. There is also something very personal about crafting them yourself. Try not to fret if this isn't your thing, as purchasing them from a respectable outlet will be equally as effective.

Casting Runes

Rune casting is a common method used in runic divination where the practitioner casts out runes. One of the main purposes of runic divination is to help practitioners in making decisions about their lives, whether that is advice on how to deal with their problems, or which approach to take when facing certain situations (Tyler, 2015). Simply put, runic divination exists to guide.

For beginners, runic divination can sound quite exciting. After all, who wouldn't want to be able to see the future? However, I would caution you to manage your expectations. As stated previously, this kind of magic doesn't give you the exact answer to your questions.

There is no one specified method to do this. However, there are some established patterns and spreads for you to try out. Make sure you had a quiet place and time to begin your reading. Any outside disturbance will cast a shadow on your inner being and add to the turmoil, leading to an inaccurate reading. You need a clear mind to focus on the subject at hand. Take deep breaths and calm your entire body and mind.

Think about any issue or question that has been nagging your mind. If you wish, you can say a silent prayer to the God or deity of your choice. Lay your rune cloth in front of you and place the runes upon it.

Just like in tarot, there are several different spreads and layouts for rune casting. But if you are trying this for the first time, go simple. Pick out one Rune and analyze it completely. If you get comfortable with a simple spread, you can then try out the other variations.

Before you place the runes on the cloth, move your hand around in the bag and shake them up. This is similar to shuffling the cards in a tarot deck. Like other divination methods, rune casting looks at all influences—past, present, and personality—to come up with a guiding light for the person. In a three-runes cast, you need to pull out three Runes from the bag, one at a time, and place them on the cloth. The first of these indicates an overall summation of your situation or issue, the second one deals with the problems you might face in the course of your action, and the third one represents what you should do to overcome these obstacles and sail through to your goal. Another kind of spread is the nine-rune layout.

In Nordic mythology, nine is considered a magical number. For this reading, shuffle your runes and take out nine of them, one by one, and scatter them on the cloth. There is no set form as to where these runes should fall. Now open your eyes and see what pattern has been formed by the runes. Which ones are facing up and down? Are some near the center of the cloth? Some might be toward the far end. See where each rune has fallen and its direction. Then interpret it, keeping in mind your past and present influencers.

As per the Runic alphabet, you will find that each symbol has more than one meaning. Therefore, experts emphasize that you should never go by the meaning provided but instead figure out the overall picture and then make an interpretation. For example, Ehwaz means "horse." It also means "wheel" or "luck." So, does that mean you are getting a horse? Or a new set of wheels? Or maybe you will get lucky? Could be. However, add that to the other runes and look at the past and present influences and personality. It could mean anything. They might have some luck in their travels. Maybe they could gallop in the wind like the horse and find their stable, i.e., their true goal. Sometimes, these three meanings can point to something even better—maybe an unexpected bonus or promotion at work!

Do not worry if you do not get satisfactory results straight away. It takes time, patience, and years of study before you can begin to understand the runes and their meanings. There are several books and online resources available to guide you in your quest. Of course, as with any other method of divination, you have to rely on your powers of intuition and deduction for a rounded analysis. And just like with tarot cards, an upside-down or sideways rune can have a completely different meaning compared to an upright rune. Make sure you consult your guide to figure out the correct meaning.

Rune stones or crystals are stored in a small pouch tied with string. The pouch is soft and keeps the runes safely in one place. Alternate means could include a rune box or a rune chest where you can keep your cloth and runes together. Make sure you clean them after every reading.

Sometimes, blank runes come in a rune set. That could leave ample room for interpretation, but traditional practitioners of the craft have said that they have never encountered anything like a blank rune in their castings. If you wish to remove them from your reading, that is fine too.

Interpreting Runes

Now that you've gotten a crash course in rune casting, you should realize that interpreting runes is no easy task. Few people are able to read runes on their first go. Runic divination is an art form, and it takes time and patience to pick up the skill.

Generally, rune sets come with some kind of instruction guide to aid beginners. There are also numerous books, blogs, and videos that you can consult if you want to begin trying runic divination.

However, learning to interpret runes is a lifelong journey. You will never be done learning. In fact, Asatru is a faith of continuous learning, reading, and knowledge. So, don't expect to sit down, cast runes, and immediately come up with answers.

Even the most experienced rune casters struggle with interpretation, and it can sometimes take weeks before the answers are revealed to them.

If you're really keen on runic divination, I would advise that you take your time and be patient. Runic divination is a complicated art and requires time more than anything else.

How Meditation Can Help with Readings

Practicing both ceremonial and casual meditation on the runes is a source of immense wisdom and a direct source of magical power. The vitki must aspire to establish a personal link with each rune by corresponding with the mystery on a deep level. Once this link has been developed with each particular rune and the entire runic cosmology, a floodgate of runic force is unlocked, creating a surge of wisdom and knowledge that always stands available to the vitki. Later this stream may be tapped even on an informal basis, in any spare time that permits reflection. On most occasions, these odd moments furnish the vitki with some of the most potent insights into the mysteries of the runic world.

Suppose you can place yourself into a higher level of thought due to meditation. There, you will immediately discover that, even if you are not actively meditating, your senses are still more aware than ever. Every time you open your senses to the everyday world, you exercise and continuously train your mind to see things differently. You will have other perspectives on where you can base your decisions.

Because you are more in tune with your surroundings, you can easily pick up the smaller details you may have otherwise missed, helping you make sense of the runes better. For instance, when you sit down with a person for a rune reading, you can get a grasp of his or her personality. You can read other people better so you can give them a more accurate interpretation of the runes.

Here is a sample scenario. You have a friend who is going for a job interview next week, and he wants to know if he will get the job. Being his friend, you already know that he is the kind of person who will tense up during an interview but is also very qualified.

You also know the job your friend is interviewing for involves dealing with other people, so it is important for him to work on his people skills. In that case, you may cast your runes. Perhaps Uruz is the most important. Uruz is a rune for power –but it is one out of people's control. It can also mean that success is nearby.

Typically, you can tell your friend that success is near, but it comes with a power he has no control over. Also, you are not sure when this power will come. If you meditate before the reading and are in a more mindful state, you can sense your friend's attitude about the job. If you feel that your friend is in control, the power without control likely comes with the job.

Runic meditation is an active, striving endeavor. One of the most vital skills required for attaining success is the control of thought, that is, submersion of thoughts damaging to the objective of meditation and guiding of the thoughts along the wild rune path. Once the hugr is calm and thought patterns gathered into a single-center, the rune insight will start to well up in the consciousness of the vitki. Runic meditation focuses on three main elements: form, sound, and root idea. The vitki should try to concentrate gently on one or all the elements included in this threefold complex, quietly steering detrimental thoughts and leaving behind only the runic symbols of form, sound, and root idea until ultimately the rune begins to communicate directly to the consciousness of the vitki.

Ceremonial runic meditation may be as intricate or as modest as the vitki wishes or is proficient at performing. Usually, it appears that the most sensible path is the one that works from simplicity towards complexity. Preparations for the process of meditation involve a serene location, proficiency in one of the protection-invocation rites, and the creation of a set of meditational cards.

Over time, mastery of the stadha of the chosen rune may be critical. In the initial stages of the meditational program, the vitki may want to focus only on one element of the threefold complex and incorporate others in accordance with the self-directed program. A wiki should develop a precise, detailed, scheme that suits their own needs and capacities. They must always pay attention to building a more affluent complex of elements in the inner center of concentration while including a comprehensive variety of magical techniques in the outer procedure.

Given below is a synthesized overview of varied methods of runic meditation from which the vitki may draw in the formation of a meditational program. All techniques may be physically conducted, or if more beneficial or effective, they may be performed entirely within the hugauga.

Perform one of the protective-invocatory rites while strongly visualizing the rune ring.

Take a comfortable stance, either sitting or standing or in the stadha of the particular rune. You may face either north, east, or in the angle specified by the rune's position in the rune ring.

A runic meditation card should be set in a proper position. It must be affixed to the wall or placed on a simple stand, positioned so that it is at eye level during this stage of the procedure.

Fix your eyes truly on the runic form depicted on the card and sing the rune galdr softly. Consecutively, if you want, you may bring up formulaic ideas, such as the name of the rune, on a secondary level of consciousness. A name is for sure included in the galdr. However, here we are contemplating the esoteric meaning embodied in the name, which may be involved in the 'center of concentration.' At this stage, the vitki should focus on seeking a sharp concentration on the elements of the runic complex.

As the next step, the vitki should shut their eyes, proceeding with the galdr and consideration of an esoteric principle. Visualize the form of the rune as it occurs on the card and in the mind's eye, and furthermore, try to realize the oneness of the form-sound-idea complex. Initially, you might have to open your eyes to reestablish the stave form. Still, ultimately you will be able to discontinue the fourth phase and begin directly to a complex inward reflection once you gain confidence in your aptitudes.

Retain this state of inner concentration on the runic complex for at least a few seconds and build up towards a period of five minutes.

After this phase of inward concentration, the vitki should fall into inner silence. But keep in mind that this is a totally attentive silence. During this void of hibernating thoughts, the word is the rune will be intoned with a resounding peal. This is a 'word' that cannot be asserted in any language, but it is the totality of the runic mystery expressed in a solitary moment. This is a holy occurrence where the rune and the vitki's hugr are unified for a moment.

The vitki may prefer to continue with the meditation as long as they feel a connection with the runic force. In this meditative state, the vitki may be led along with some rune paths, in which secrets regarding the rune itself are disclosed, or the associations between certain runes are made apparent-the possibilities are countless.

Once the connection breaks up, or the vitki wishes to discontinue the meditation, repeat a formula as 'Now the work is wrought' and open your eyes. After that, ritually break the rune ring in accordance with the rules of the hammer rite.

Later, when you feel yourself actually becoming a part of the rune world, additional informal meditational procedures may be attempted. These meditational undertakings will unearth a substantial amount of both applicable and fascinating wisdom and knowledge. It has been discovered that the most helpful tools in this venture are paper, pen, compass, protractor, and maybe even a calculator. The process is quite simple: Position yourself at your writing desk or table, surrounded by several runic glyphs and cosmological configurations. Steady your mind, turning it toward the rune world.

Enable your hugr to drift away until it gleams on a seed concept, then relentlessly follow it, drawing and noting down your 'revelations' as they come to you. These notes can later serve as the ground for additional work-they will not frequently be prospects for the round file. It is perhaps best not to plan these informal sessions but instead to sit down and delve into the mysteries when 'the spirit moves you.' Generally, after a brief amount of time, the wisdom of the runes will start to well up in the hugr of the vitki at odd moments. Occasionally the surge of these forces is so strong as to cause psychokinetic phenomena in the physical proximity of the vitki!

The periodic practice of runic meditation is one of the mainstays in the all-around rigging of rune wisdom that gives adequate rewards for efforts well spent.

Incorporating Norse Magic into Daily Life

Just as the Germanic tribes incorporated Norse magic into their daily lives, we can do the same today. To the Old Norse, magic was knowledge, as large a part of their life as possessing agrarian skills or battle skills.

Norse magic has always been a way to understand one's place in the world and a way to create the life you want to live through your own will. Magic could guide your life and help you control it. While this is important today, it was even more important during the Iron Age and the age of the Vikings. There was always much to question. Using magic rituals to uncover your fate, make plans to change that which was ordained by the Norns was crucial. Knowing what fate had planned, you could respond in an honorable way to any challenges or even devise ways to influence or affect your life's preordained plan.

With that in mind, Norse magic was then and is now a way to add a layer of control and understanding to your life. The Norse people did not view their fate as something that would prevent them from exercising their free will. They believed that you could aid and construct your will to best benefit the situations ahead. There was a certain sense of freedom in not having to guess your preordained future life. Within those constraints, you could achieve great things. Magic was a way to enhance their ability to do just that.

Today, the use of magic easily coincides with our desire to self-actualize, to accept where we are in life, and work to make our lives better. Magic was always a way to frame and respond to challenges, which in the time of the Vikings were many. Today, we have modern medicine and healthcare and the guidance of education. Yet the appeal and strength of magic are still very strong. Norse magic was one of the earliest recorded ways humans attempted to better control their lives and understand that the world was more than just themselves.

Magic helped the people who practiced it to protect themselves against evil, successfully handle illness, and attempt to improve relationships, both personal ones and with the land itself. With the focus on survival being both successes in battle and an agrarian life and many farmsteads and family groups isolated from one another, it was through the practice of magic, the knowledge of skilled magic practitioners, and the faith in magic's healing properties that communities could unite.

Magic was not only the knowledge of the mystical and the natural worlds, but it was also based on practical wisdom. The runic alphabet grew in use and from the desire to invoke magic. Magic led to literacy and understanding of the "other" which is located beyond the most provincial and small groups.

CHAPTER 9: AETTIR

The origins of this organization are unclear, and many artifacts that bear inscriptions of the full Elder Futhark represent the runes in one row that goes horizontal, rather than having the three rows of eight at all. But other inscriptions will show it split up in this way. It may just be a way for some people to learn it faster than in the past, but it also may just be something that we did in our modern times.

Each of the Aettir, or the families, will be named after one of the gods associated with the first rune in that particular row. So, in our first row, we have the symbol of Fehu, and it is known as the Freyr's Aett or the Frey's Aett. Then we have the second row, which is supposed to have the symbol of Hagalaz, which gives us Hagal's Aett (sometimes called Heimdall's Aett). Then we can end with the Tyr's Aett, which is made up in the third row and will begin with the symbol of Tiwaz.

These divisions make it so much easier for us to learn and then memorize some of the shapes found in our runes, but they will also create some patterns of relationships among the runes that we can use for our magical purposes what we hope to do. For example, we can also look at the connection between the second runes that fall in each set to help us out here.

These will include the symbols of Uruz, Nauthiz, and Berkana, and we can focus on what each one is all about. The Uruz is all about being with brute strength, and then Nauthiz is all about strong need. We can then end here with Berkana, which is the birth rune, both on a literal level of giving birth and a symbolic level of something new happening to you.

Anyone familiar with childbirth, for example, knows that there is a good deal of strength that is needed to deliver successfully. Still, this combination can sometimes speak to the need for giving rise to the birth of a new idea that lends great strength to an enterprise or a project, for example, the relationships that come up between these runes and the specific situation that the person reading them will have going on in their past will help you to read them a bit better.

Frey – The Mother

Frey is the first group or family, which symbolizes fertility. It is the reason it is also classified as the Mother. It serves as the vital force together with the way it is demonstrated inside the human body. It is also about awakening your consciousness. As the first Aett, the Frey signifies the first few steps you have to take for your enlightened future. This means it is something you should track to reach your ultimate goal.

Heimdall – The Warrior

The God, Heimdall, leads this second division. He is viewed as the God of silence sometimes, which others also perceive as priestly meditation. In essence, though, Heimdall can be considered a warrior. He is a watchful warrior, capable of facing struggles and dealing with overwhelming odds. It is in his watchfulness wherein he shows endless courage.

Tyr – The King

This group, which can also be viewed as the King, shows people's relationship with the divine forces. It also encompasses the roles they play in fate. This aett also refers to the human condition. It symbolizes social aspects and men and women's spiritual transformation.

Freyr's Aett

Fehu ᚠ: "Cattle/Wealth"

Fehu is the first rune in The Elder Futhark. It represents prosperity and material wealth, income won or earned, good luck abundance, and prosperity ahead, both financial and social. If read reversed, it may reveal a potential loss, either personal or financial.

Uruz ᚢ: "Ox"

Uruz, the stone of endurance, perseverance, and motivation represents a wild bull. It reveals energy, courage, health, endurance, speed, power, and masculinity. If reversed, it may show losses of strength or health or the control of others over you.

Thurisaz ᚦ: "Mallet/Giant"

Representing a large hammer, possibly Thor's hammer, or a giant, this rune reveals powerful energy, challenges, and defense. It could also represent a purge and catharsis. Reversed: danger, conflict, destruction, betrayal. As such, it indicates a powerful direction of energy and force for either destruction or defense, so it may also indicate conflict.

Ansuz ᚨ: "Message"

Representing communication, a message, or an arriving

insight, it can be read as a divine messenger, a revelation, good advice, and inspiration. When reversed, it can indicate deceit or misunderstandings.

Raidho ᚱ: "Journey"

The rune for a wheel or vehicle such as a chariot, Raidho indicates a move or journey, either physical or spiritual. It signifies progress, evolution, and increased perspective. When reversed, it can signify disruption or the lack of justice.

Kenaz ᚲ: "Torch"

This rune represents a flame or torch, and one's own personal light, revealing unknown facts, guidance, secrets, and even enlightenment, such as a true calling or inspiration. Reversed: it may reveal being stuck in place, instability, and a lack of comprehension.

Gebo ᚷ: "Gift"

Gebo is the symbol of gifts. It reveals generosity, blessings, talents, and happy relationships. There is no reverse reading, making this rune itself a true, positive gift.

Wunjo ᚹ: "Joy"

Wunjo reveals victory, triumph, celebration, a feast, and harmony, as well as joyous occasions. In reverse, it can indicate sorrow and loss.

Heimdall's Aett (Talisa and Sam, n.d.)

Moving on to Heimdall's Aett, this second set of the runic alphabet is that of the watchman of the gods.

Hagalaz ᚺ: "Hail"

Hagalaz stands for hail, and for a change or test that is disruptive but out of our control. Just how destructive it is depends on our own ability to handle this type of change or storm, to grow through our own hardship or mistakes. Like hail itself, which will melt, this adversity will pass. As with the rune for Gebo, there is no inverted meaning.

Nauthiz ᚾ: "Needs"

Nauthiz reveals that which is necessary to us, both emotionally and for work and survival. Understanding our own needs helps us to care for ourselves. The rune indicates a need for endurance and the ability to handle restrictions. Read in reverse it reveals the potential for distress and depression.

Isa ᛁ: "Ice"

Representing ice, Isa is about taking a pause, a sense of stillness, and waiting. It may be the delay we need or it can be the frustration or blockage we must overcome. There is no inverted meaning to this rune.

Jera ᛃ: "Harvest"

Representing the harvest, this rune is about abundance, reaping what you sow, a conclusion in the cycle of life. It also indicates the potential for a positive breakthrough. There is no inverted meaning to this rune, either.

Eihwaz ᛇ: "Yew"

Representing the yew tree, also known as Yggdrasil, Eihwaz signifies The Tree of Life. When cast, it reveals survival, a steadfast endurance, knowledge, and inspiration, as well as reliability, purpose, and a sense of enlightenment. In reverse, it can indicate confusion and even destruction.

Perthro ᛈ: "Destiny"

The rune of gamblers and diviners, literally stands for fortune, as it represents a dice cup. It reveals the chance of life, a sense of fate and mystery, risk, and even a game. It can also represent female fertility; after all, conceiving and bearing a child is certainly a part of risk and destiny. It also indicates the need to play your hand, accept change, and look for meaning and secrets. When reversed in a reading, it may reveal a loss of faith and purpose, standing still.

Algiz ᛉ: "Elk"

The rune for elk, Algiz, reveals both protection and defense when it is cast. It is a guardian, courage, power and guidance, and a shield against evil. In reverse, it can stand for a hidden challenge or danger.

Sowilo ᛋ: "Sun"

Representing the sun, Sowilo indicates joy, success, inspiration, good luck, and justice. With no inverted meaning, it reveals a time to celebrate health, power, and successes of all kinds.

Hagal or Heimdall's Aett

Hagal's Aett, or Heimdall's Aett, is the second aett in the Elder Futhark. This aett is associated with the chaotic and often unexpected things that we face in life.

Because little is known about Hagalaz, many associate this aett with Heimdall, the guardian God of Asgard. He protects his realm from all destructible forces that appear with the warning of his horn.

Hagalaz

Also known as Hagalas, Hagal, Hagl, Haal

Sounds like "Ha-ga-lahz"

Letter sound: H

Literal translation: hail

Symbolizes hail, destruction, disruption, chaos, misfortune

Hagalaz is the rune of hail. Hail represents the destructive force of nature. It comes on strong, out of nowhere sometimes, and then it passes. You can't control your circumstances just as you can't control nature.

Whether it's a literal hail storm, an illness, or some other unexpected chaos that arises in your life, you're often left damaged. This rune can be an indication that your progress is hindered. This could be your progress at work, on a personal creative project, spiritual growth, or anything else. If the surrounding runes cast are positive, this could mean whatever obstacle you're facing is a small setback and nothing life-altering. However, if the surrounding runes cast are negative, it could imply that these obstacles are serious and long-term.

The important thing to remember is that hail is temporary. It will pass, and soon the small ice chunks will be nothing but a puddle of water that dries up in the sun.

Nauthiz

Also known as Nauth, Nod, Nied, Nautiz, Naudirz

Sounds like "NAW-theez"

Letter sound: N

Literal Translation: need

Symbolizes need necessity, scarcity, absence, restriction

Nauthiz is the rune of needs. The symbol of the rune is

based on a ritual fire that was lit from two large pieces of wood when the ancient Norse people would experience disaster. It signifies how their needs were being compromised.

This rune could mean your physical needs aren't being met, such as hunger, unemployment, or poor health. It could also be that your mental health is lacking. Perhaps you're feeling lonely or don't have any emotional support. This can prevent you from moving forward in life. At the time, it seems impossible to fix, but these hardships can be a good thing. You can use them to learn and grow. At the time you're facing these obstacles, it's hard, but in the long run, you'll look back and know you made it. Then, you'll face another hardship, but you'll have the wisdom of your previous experience to guide you through it. Hardship is necessary for growth.

As you wait for these hardships to pass, it's a struggle. This rune could be an indication that you need to have patience until you're able to move forward.

Alternatively, this rune could be warning you to avoid greed, which leads to harmful behavior. If you're focused so much on your wants, you compromise your integrity to get it. Leave the material world behind. Forget about your ego and focus on what really matters—what you really need.

Isa

Also known as Eis, Iss, Isaz, Is, Isarz

Sounds like "EE-sah"

Letter sound: I (as in ice)

Literal translation: ice

Symbolism is ice, frozen, obstacles, delay, stagnant

Isa is the rune of ice. Ice is frozen, which could represent a lack of movement both physically and mentally. Maybe you've been too exhausted lately to pursue your goals. Perhaps it means that you're unable to move forward mentally as if facing "writer's block" for your mind.

Though you may be standing still at a time when you want to move forward, it's best to accept your reality as it is instead of fighting it. Take this time to work toward your progress and prepare for when you're able to move forward again. Just remember, eventually, the sun will thaw the ice. During this time, use meditation to clear your mind and focus. Because ice is clear, this could represent gaining clarity of a situation.

Alternatively, it could represent the 'coldness' between you and another person. Your relationship with someone may be losing its 'heat' and your affection for one another is dwindling. You may need a cooling off period to think clearly. Maybe this "cooling off" will fix things, or maybe it will result in the end of a relationship.

Jera

Also known as Jer, Jara, Jeran, Jeraz, Gaar, Ar

Sounds like "yare-ah"

Letter sound: Y

Literal Translation: year

Symbolism is the year, harvest, cycle, natural, fertility, growth, reward

Jera is the rune of the year. As the seasons pass, it results in the harvest. This rune represents growth in the sense that in the spring, you plant the seed. Then, with hard work, you watch it grow until it's finally ready to be harvested. This is why the rune also represents reward. With hard work, you reap the rewards of the harvest. At this point, you'll begin to prepare for the winter as the cycle continues.

Many paths follow the Wheel of the Year, which is a Pagan wheel that represents the cycle of life. Each cycle has its own meaning and purpose, just as the seasons do. Casting this rune could remind you to be patient. It takes time to fulfill your goals. You can't plant a seed and expect it to grow into a plant overnight. It takes months of hard work, but your perseverance will pay off.

Alternatively, if you've been struggling, this rune could indicate that the tough times are almost over and the future's looking bright.

Eihwaz

Also known as Eoh, Eihuaz, Aihs, Ihwaz

Sounds like "eye-wahz"

Letter sound: ae (as in eye)

Literal Translation: Yew tree

Symbolism is Yew, death, rebirth, changes

Eihwaz represents the Yew tree. Yew is toxic to humans and animals. In ancient times, people would use it for poison. Whether through murder or suicide, yew could kill anyone who ingests it. In fact, it can also poison anyone who simply drinks from a cup that was made from wood as every part of the tree is poisonous.

Though, death linked with this rune doesn't need to be literal. Death could also mean a change is coming. It's the end of one thing and the beginning of another, like when you hear "one door closes and another opens."

This could symbolize the 'death' of a relationship, a career, or even a way of life. Perhaps you're leaving behind your old ways to grow spiritually. In this sense, it could be a symbol of rebirth. Yew is also in the middle of Elder Futhark, meaning that death is not the end. Because it's in the middle, it shows the possibility to continue after death.

After all, Yew is considered a tree of life. Ironically, a chemical in the bark has been used for medical treatment. Not to mention, Yggdrasil was possibly a Yew tree. It can also live for thousands of years, proving its powerful force of life.

Perthro

Also known as Perth, Peorth, Peordh, Perdhro, Perthra, Perthu

Sounds like "per-throw"

Letter sound: P

Literal translation: Dice cup

Symbolism is cup, games, chance, fate, unknown, mystery, destiny

Perthro is possibly the most controversial among the runes. That's because scholars have a difficult time agreeing on the meaning.

People often used dice cups for games of chance, leaving their fate in the hands of the universe. For this reason, fate holds a lot of meaning for this rune. While it isn't always clear why life unfolds the way it does, there's a purpose to these seemingly random events. Fate is a mystery until it's revealed.

One lesson that Perthro teaches us about fate is that it's not always black and white. You can look at fate and think that one ending is 'good' and another is 'bad.' but the truth is that it's so complex, there is no simple category to file one's fate under.

However, you can gauge how fate might affect you. If the other runes cast with it are negative, it could indicate disappointment is waiting for you. If that's the case, you might want to hold off on taking risks—don't gamble your money.

Because of its mysterious nature, Perthro could indicate that a secret is about to be revealed. This could be a secret that someone close to you has kept, or even a spiritual truth revealing itself to you. Pay attention to any signs you might notice and get in tune with the spiritual energies surrounding you.

In contrast, it could indicate a secret you're holding onto. It could be something from your past that you struggle to let go of. Casting this rune might be telling you that holding onto this secret is damaging, and you should look within to find the answers to whatever troubles are plaguing you.

Algiz

Also known as Elhaz, Eolh, Elgr

Sounds like "AL-geez"

Letter sound: Z

Literal translation: Elk

Symbolizes protection, defense, opportunity

Algiz is the rune of the elk. This represents protection as the elk's massive antlers protect it from predators. For this reason, casting this rune indicates you're safe from danger. However, it doesn't imply you should live with reckless behavior. Despite its indication of safety, you should always stay alert to trouble and potential threats. Let the divine guide you so the moves you make keep you from harm.

Alternatively, this rune could indicate that you're losing touch with your intuition. Your intuition is what keeps you safe, even if not in a physical sense. It allows you to see when someone is taking advantage of you or trying to harm you emotionally. If you're not connected with your spiritual side, you leave yourself vulnerable to attack.

Sowilo

Also known as Sigel, Sol, Sunna, Sowulu

Sounds like "so-WEE-lo"

Letter sound: S

Literal Translation: sun

Symbolism is victory, light, energy, enlightenment, success

Sowilo is the rune of the sun. The sun provides nourishment and light. Darkness can obscure our vision, even in the spiritual sense. If you're feeling darkness within, this rune might indicate that you need to open yourself to the light and allow it to claim victory over the darkness.

This applies when the darkness comes from others. If someone is trying to harm you emotionally, keep yourself focused on the light as the light allows you clarity. When you have light, you can see everything around you better. The light promotes optimism and enlightenment.

Tyr's Aett

The god, Tyr, represents protection and complete victory. He is also the symbol of cosmic justice and all the things that relate to the politics of rulership. This aett concerns itself with intellect, spiritual growth, and understanding without judgment.

If you get a majority of the runes belonging to Tyr's aett during a casting session, then it could indicate that you are too inactive in achieving your goals. It could be you are overthinking your moves, or you are not centered because you are still uncertain of what you want.

Tir/Teiwaz

Sound: "t"

The first rune in Tyr's aett is coincidentally named after God itself or at least a version of his name. It represents victory and justice, just like the deity. It is also called the Creator's rune.

Just like Sowilo, casting Tir usually promises success in your endeavor, but it may require you to make a personal sacrifice. Whether you will make a sacrifice or not will be the catalyst for your success. This rune also works well when embroiled in sticky legal matters, but only if you are in the right.

Just like the beginning of Heimdall's aett, Tyr's aett begins with a loss. However, it is a sacrifice you will do voluntarily. Unlike the hail sent down by the gods, the loss you will experience at the beginning of the third aett is under your control. You can get through without the sacrifice indicated, but this will be difficult.

However, to gain the benefits from the succeeding runes, make that sacrifice. Just like when Tyr had to sacrifice one of his hands so Fenrir, the gigantic and powerful wolf that was said to bring forth Ragnarok, could be shackled.

When you get a reversed casting of Tir, the consequences

include loss of self-confidence, becoming an untrustworthy person in the eyes of your peers, and cowardice. In other words, you become the type of person who is weak, not just physically but mentally, and emotionally.

As mentioned earlier, this rune may help you sway the judge's favor toward your side, so carve its symbol on a small piece of wood. It should be small enough to fit in your pocket. You should then bring it with you to the courthouse.

Berkano/Berhano

Sound: "b"

This rune represents the Birch Tree. It represents a new beginning, like a birch coming to life from a similar tree from a seed buried in the soil. Berkano represents fertility and having a home in complete peace and harmony. If you are planning to have a new member of your family, you can strive to gain the blessing of this rune.

It is also the perfect rune when trying to deal with concealment and secrecy. If you have something private and you wish to keep it that way, you may find the power of Berkano useful. The reason is that it ensures that you or anyone else will be spreading your secret around for everyone to see.

The Berkano is primarily oriented towards the feminine.

However, you will notice it looks like a pair of breasts. It is a nurturing rune as indicative of it being oriented towards femininity. You can expect healing in both the physical and spiritual manner.

When cast in the negative, Berkano can cause secrecy within all household members, immaturity, and lust instead of fertility. In the worst-case scenario, a reversed Berkano may also signify abandonment.

To use this rune, you can carve it into a bedpost of a couple trying to conceive. You will also find it useful when placed in barnyard stalls where livestock are expected to bear their young.

Ehwaz

Sound: "e" as it sounds in "every"

Ehwaz represents the twin gods, the Alcis. You can often picture it as two brothers on horseback and linked by a wooden beam. This beam symbolizes the strong partnership between the twin brothers. It means that one cannot move without the cooperation of the other.

The rune Ehwaz is the Norse symbol for the horse, which represents partnership. As such, it deals with anything that concerns partnerships, like marriage, relationships, and business relations. Appealing to this rune will strengthen the bonds between the partners.

Casting this rune also means a new journey. For instance, you may be due for a job change soon or discover that you will need to move to a new home because of a job transfer. Just like the rune Tir, Ehwaz signifies a new start, but it may involve giving up something in return.

Another meaning you can divine when you cast Ehwaz is following the natural flow of a task you have in hand. It means learning how to work well with others instead of constantly butting heads. It also indicates learning how to depend on others, making it possible for you to accomplish all your tasks.

This rune's reversal may denote a couple of negative things, like treachery and reckless haste in doing tasks, which often end in disaster. It could also mean breaking up standing partnerships.

In neo-pagan unions, the couple would paint the rune Ehwaz on their hands as a symbol of their everlasting partnership. They also do so as to proof of trust and loyalty toward each other. And you can carve this rune on a plaque and hang it above your headboard.

Mannaz

Sound: "m"

It is the rune that symbolizes humankind. It can either represent your race or just you, the individual. This rune is incredibly special. You can apply it to situations and purposes that serve a social nature. It also helps strengthen bonds between the members of a group and develop a rational mind to deal with squabbles.

Casting Mannaz means undergoing self-analysis and inward reflection. If you find yourself stuck on a task and cannot seem to figure out what you need to do to advance, you can cast it hoping to find the answers to your questions. Mannaz may also indicate the need to work on your personal reputation and people skills. Casting Mannaz when you have trouble working with other people may represent your desire to improve yourself instead of trying to find fault in the other members of your group. On the other hand, it can also mean you and your team have a strong bond with each other, and there is nothing you can't do when you work together.

Now, when Mannaz is in the negative, it may mean there will be a small problem that gets blown way out of proportion, negatively affecting your partnership. There are also instances when it signifies that you are unwittingly sabotaging your relationship and that your bond is getting weaker by the day.

You will do well to inscribe this symbol on your dinner table as that is where you and your family usually discuss family matters. It will amplify the bond you and your family share, leading to productive discussions.

Laguz

Sound: "l"

This rune represents the element of water and its flowing nature. It symbolizes the sheer power of water as well as its ability to follow the path of least resistance when it is flowing. Laguz is also symbolic of human thought and how you need to use it for good.

When you get Laguz from your rune casting, one way to read it is a safe harbor or place that offers you sanctuary from all the negativity in the world. Alternatively, it may not even be a place. It may symbolize a supportive partner or harmonious relationship you can count on when troubled.

Drawing a Laguz also indicates you were right to follow your intuition regarding any of the tasks at hand. Just like the flow of water, you let your intuition guide you toward the right path. You did not need to overthink and come up with your own obstacles. Laguz means you should let your unconscious mind take over occasionally as it may come up with a better idea.

A Laguz positioned in reversal, on the other hand, may indicate that you are emotionally manipulated, either by someone else who is close to you or even yourself. It could happen when you come up with excuses not to do something that is supposed to benefit you in the long run.

Carving this rune into an amulet or anything similar can aid in the further advancement of your mental abilities. It means you can learn even more. Another benefit of having a Laguz effect is that it can further enhance your intuition, making you much better at making decisions.

Inguz/Ing

Sound: "ng" as in the word "long"

Inguz is the Rune of Sexuality, which means it has power over physical attraction toward others, and ultimately, sex. This rune affects sex, but Inguz is only mostly concerned with the act in terms of reproduction and fertility.

Casting Inguz also means having the ability to spread your energy as far as you want to. It makes it possible for you to influence more people or provide more individuals with protection. However, to use the power of Inguz properly, it is important to build up your energy over time. Once you reach a certain level, you release it all at once.

During a reading, getting Inguz may also indicate the need to use more of your common sense during decision-making if you tend to follow suit with what everyone else around you is doing without considering what could happen to you.

Seeing this rune can help you figure out if you have to step back and use your common sense to realize that you are on the wrong path.

There is nothing much to worry about if you get a reversed Inguz rune during your casting, as it usually deals with minor inconveniences such as lust and immaturity. However, it may also signify decreased libido or infertility.

You can use Inguz in many ways aside from rune casting. For instance, you can carve the symbol on a piece of wood that is small enough to keep in your pocket. It will increase your chances of attracting a mate. You can also carve this rune on your bedpost to improve your sex life.

Dagaz

Sound: "d"

Dagaz, also known as the Rune of Transformation, represents a huge transformation, which might be of the spiritual, mental, or social type. Also called the Rune of Daybreak, it signifies the change between night and day, which is vast, to say the least. If you are seeking guidance when you need to make an important decision, Dagaz is one of the runes that can help.

Casting Dagaz also denotes the need to reconsider your current circumstance and whether you need to make a drastic change. It means you are questioning whether your decision is correct or not.

Another meaning you can get from Dagaz during a casting session is the stability between opposing forces, such as light and darkness. You are getting hints on whether you need to certainly adjust to attain balance in your life.

The good thing about this rune is that it rarely has reverse effects. However, if the Dagaz rune gets surrounded by opposing, reversed runes, it could mean you have to look forward. You may also have to stop dwelling on the past too much.

Because Dagaz is the Rune of Transformation, it would work well when inscribed on the doors of a school or any other learning institution. Better yet, you should be able to find it in rehabilitation centers because those who are checked in want to transform into much better versions of themselves.

Othala/Othila

Sound: "o" like in "old"

Othala is the Rune of Loyalty, which represents fealty to one's family, clan, tribe, country, or even cause/belief. Like Fehu, Othala is symbolic of wealth. However, unlike Fehu, Othala's wealth is intangible. This wealth is family, culture, heritage, and friendships. Othala represents a kind of enclosure and a way of maintaining the status quo.

Getting this rune during a reading usually connotes issues regarding your ancestry birthright. For instance, there may be something big going on in your hometown you would do well to at least inquire about.

This rune may also signify something related to your immediate family. For instance, a sibling of yours may want to reconnect after many years of not speaking. Another meaning might be that you will be called upon by your country or culture to lend your skills, like enlisting in the military. You may also work toward protecting your heritage soon.

Now, the most obvious negative effect of this rune is developing racism, bigotry, and general xenophobia. One unfortunate instance of the use of this rune was during World War II when Othala was engraved in the knives issued to the Hitler Youth members. Should you want to use this rune to gain its energy, you have to do so aided by something connected to family matters, like a family crest.

Odin's Rune

In modern use, the optional blank rune, known as Odin's

Rune, may be included in runes used for divination. As such, if cast, reveals that we do not yet have all the answers we seek, but this lack of knowledge is still acceptable.

One of the primary teachings of the Norse Faith is the concept of Wyrd. That means that everything in the cosmos is interconnected, resulting in the actions one takes (or doesn't take) potentially impacting not only this person's life but the lives of others, whether they are present around them or not. True to the concept of Wyrd, respect for nature should be inherent. Norse Pagans are environmentally aware and recognize that for our Earth to remain bountiful, we must care for it and nurture it.

Aside from the usual 24 runes that compose the Futhark runic alphabet, modern neo-pagans and heathenry practitioners have introduced an extra blank tile in their rune sets and gave it the name Wyrd, which means fate.

Total emptiness or infinite possibilities? Depending on how you look at it, there are many ways through which you can read Odin's rune. This rune was a later addition by modern neo-pagans to get some additional chance from the cosmos when casting runes. Users of this rune say that when Odin's rune appears in your cast, it means that the unknown is at work and it is there even if you cannot see it.

Even though many rune casters use Odin's rune these days, its actual meaning is still hotly debated. Some say it means endless possibilities, while others say it indicates emptiness. It is like the glass half-full or half-empty conundrum.

What Does the Blank Rune Mean?

Whenever you get a blank rune, take note it could signify that you ran into some complications with your casting. It may be a hint that your inquiry is not worded properly, or it may be that the answer you are seeking is impossible to grasp (or maybe deep inside, you already know the answer). Take it as a sign you need to meditate and wait for before giving your reading another shot.

The consensus about Odin's rune is there is none. If you ask ten people about it, you will also get ten answers. There is no one definition of the blank rune. Any potential user can use it on whatever day they want to.

In his book "A Handbook for the Use of an Ancient Oracle" (1983), Ralph Blum said that the appearance of the blank rune is an omen of death. However, that death might just be symbolic and not an actual passing of a person. It can also refer to a certain part of your life gone and replaced by another.

According to Lisa Peschel, author of "A Practical Guide to the Runes: Their Uses in Divination and Magick," whenever this rune appears, the only thing you can expect is that something unexpected will happen to you. This something can be positive or negative depending on whether you have been virtuous. It is also best to interpret its meaning by basing it on how it relates to its neighbors.

Kylie Holmes, the author of "Pagan Portals: Runes" (2013), said that casting the blank rune indicates there is progress in your spiritual development. This act also reminds you how large your knowledge is. It is bigger compared to how other people view it.

In over a millennium of its existence, there have been very few modifications to the runic alphabet. These variations are usually geographic, and the shapes of certain runes were the only notable changes. Their meanings remained the same. However, there has been a modern addition to the Elder and Younger Futhark runic alphabet, and it is the Wyrd rune.

There has been no solid evidence that the Wyrd (also called Odin's rune) existed before the resurgence of using runes, and its origins are muddy, to say the least, but even so, it is included in most rune sets these days.

What Makes the Wyrd Rune Different from the Rest?

The Wyrd rune is often just a blank tile in the set, but some say it looks like this:

This rune symbol represents all the rune shapes molded into one. According to old beliefs, it is possible to make this rune by yourself aided by clay or any similar material. Regardless of your chosen material, it would be necessary for you to get a tiny pinch of material from the other runes to produce a new and blank one. It is the blank rune that serves as the culmination of all other runes' powers.

The blank rune differs from the others in the sense it does not belong in the three Aettir of the Elder Futhark. It is only a modern addition that originated around 40 years ago in the 1980s when the New Age revolution was just taking over Western culture. However, even though it is a new addition to the runic alphabet, most modern rune casters still widely accept it.

The blank rune is also distinguishable from the rest of the runic alphabet because it is mainly a part of an ancient alphabet. This means that except for Wyrd, every rune represents a sound or combination of sounds. Some practitioners say that Wyrd represents silence, making it a unique concept since you can find no alphabet in the world with a symbol for silence.

Traditional beliefs also indicate that blank runes existed for the sole reason of having a replacement tile if a loss occurs or misplacement of another tile. Purists also believe that the blank rune does not fit into the runes' mathematical and mystical system. The reason is that you can't merely divide 25 tiles into four (four seasons in a year, four cardinal directions, and others).

The Wyrd rune does not have its own set of definitions. You can even view it as total emptiness or infinite possibilities. Some also view it as a sign of unseen forces moving in the background to affect your fate.

Why Is It Called Odin's Rune?

Another name for the Wyrd rune is Odin's rune, as it has unfathomable and mysterious power and meaning. Odin is the All-Father, the ruler of all the gods of Asgard, and yet he did not stop his quest for more knowledge. You can associate the blank rune with Odin, not only because of his omnipotence but also due to his constant hunger for more knowledge.

When Odin appears before you during a reading, he is calling out to you to look deep within yourself to achieve a deeper, more profound understanding of yourself and your being. The blank rune represents the human's almost unlimited potential, and it will be up to the reader how to take this knowledge.

It is also one reason Odin's rune does not belong in the Aettir. Odin stands alone, separate from the other aesir. Bringing any further meaning to Odin's rune would be like trying to tie a string around all the Nine Worlds. It would be futile and impossible.

How Should You Read the Blank Rune?

Although not all rune casters believe that the blank rune should be included in any rune sets, there is nothing that prevents you from using it if you want to. If you want to use Odin's rune in your readings, here are a couple of suggestions on how you can read it.

The early Anglo-Saxons, and many of the other tribal races hailing from present Northern Europe, believed in the universal force called Orlog, which means both "doom" and "destiny." Orlog oversees the fates of all the nations and their citizens. One way to read the blank rune is to base it on the concept of Orlog. This means that your individual fate is bestowed upon you by the Norns if you pull this rune.

The blank rune might mean you have karmic debt, and the cosmos is collecting payment. Now, your karmic debt might not be due to your past personal actions but from your past life. This may seem like it is unfair that you are responsible for what you did in your past life, but then again, it will also be the case for your next life. With that in mind, drawing the blank rune may mean you need to do better in your present life.

Another possible definition of the blank rune may be that you have reached a certain point in your life where you have reached the point of no return. You are destined to a singular fate soon, and you do nothing to change it. Even though you still have free will, it will not matter whatever you do now. The results will still be the same.

Now, if you pull out the blank rune in response to a specific question, it means it is not the right time for your query. It is like a Magic 8-ball telling you you should try asking again later. The cosmic fates may still cook something up for that part of your fate, so it will not register in the runes just yet. Another definition you can get from the blank rune is that you will be experiencing huge changes in your life. However, because of the ambiguous nature of the blank rune, you cannot be sure if the change will be positive or negative. It could be getting a huge promotion and raise at work or losing a family member. You need to be careful if you seem to get a huge change in your life.

Should You Use the Wyrd Rune?

It totally depends on you if you want to keep the blank rune in your rune set. Purists might scoff at you behind your back if you use this rune. Some may even find it blasphemous that you even think of using a rune that was not a part of the Elder Futhark. However, using the blank rune will provide you with one that represents nothingness and how it can affect your life.

Also, remember that not everyone is as accepting of the blank rune, especially the purists, who see it as a sacrilegious abomination. They view the blank rune as an unwelcome product of the New Age lightheadedness and the ravenous appetite for sacred symbols. For them, a rune is a symbol, not an absence of it. A symbol for the absence of a symbol is not a concept used by the Norse. It is an oxymoron, and it contradicts itself.

However, despite many people rejecting the concept of the blank rune, it will be going nowhere soon. It is an idea ingrained in neo-paganism for 40 years. Through all that time, it has been enduring continuous scrutiny and dismissals from the community. It has become such a fixture it compels rune makers who choose not to add it to their sets for sale to mention it on their labeling. It happened even though the original set of 24 runes did not have it, and it was only introduced in the 1980s.

The question remains, should you use the blank rune? The final answer will always depend on you. If you want your rune readings to be as close to the ancient traditional rune reading, then avoid using the blank tile. If you are open to possibilities and are like many of the New Age neo-pagans, then there is nothing wrong with using the blank rune in your set. You can try using it when doing readings on yourself to discover if it fits into your reading style.

Now that you know what it is, how it came to be, and how to use it, you can form your own opinion about it. Whether you use it or not, it will not change that it is already in the mainstream rune reading scene and may continue to do so for quite a long time.

CHAPTER 10: THE RUNEMASTER'S TOOLS

People treat their friends with respect, care and tend to get attached to them, leading to a long-term relationship. In the same sense, runes are like a person's friends and close allies, and therefore they need to be treated with utter care and respect. It is always profitable to maintain a good relationship with runes, as they tend to make your life better. When you craft your rune set, it should be done with care and love.

A person should never give, exchange or lend their runes to anyone. The runes that a person has crafted lovingly are for that person's use only. Lending it or exchanging would mean that the holder does not admire them as their very own. When people form their runic creations, they fill them with their own energy and force. They instill a part of themselves in their runic crafts. And these runic objects have the sole purpose of serving these people's interests and purposes. Though you can share your creative crafts with others for a short period of time, most people don't prefer that. For them, their runic board is just for their own religious, magical, and divinatory purposes.

Often, friends or acquaintances or even strangers (people who have experienced the efficacy of runes) might suggest you have a reading done. Some people tend to sway under such conditions. It is okay to choose the best suitable path. You have to realize that you are not required to justify your personal reasons to others for not lending them or letting them use your creation.

Some people have trouble maintaining boundaries, which might result in the end of your relationship with that person. Some become a nuisance and put illogical statements forward to explain why they are dearly attached to their own runes. You are not required to pay heed to these people - you can easily ignore them and move forward in life. Not everyone would understand the value of that little piece of wood (or other material) you have filled with your life energy and force.

Runic symbols can be made with a variety of different natural materials. Runes should only be touched by the person who owns them and will use them in the future. Runes can be made with pebbles, wood material, stone, and even clay. You can model runes according to your preference. Any material would suit you, depending on how you treat your runes. You can paint symbols on your wooden or clay runes in any color. Their goal is to serve your needs and your desires, and your purpose is to treat them with utmost care and respect.

Though you can design runes in any material available in nature, the most commonly used material for runic creation is wood. Wooden runes have their own charm. Although wood is a preferred choice, wooden runes do not survive a long life. There are very few runes that are present to enlighten us in today's time. Some of the oldest runes examples in Old Norse are STAFR (stave, letter, or secret lore), TEINN (twig, talismanic word for divination), and HLUTR (lot for divination, talismanic object).

In some Germanic tribes, fruitwood has been used to inscribe symbols of the runic system. The writings of famous Latin writer Tacitus have proved this factual. But, some other sources reported that those strips of runic symbols were actually crafted from ash. Both these sources could be correct. The material used matters less than the personal meaning of the rune for the individual. It is recommended that you have a personally meaningful relationship with the material to feel closer to the divine energy.

The set of runes would be more fulfilling if its material is more personalized. The decision of choosing the material for inscribing runic symbols can be based on a variety of factors. Some might choose a certain tree because they know the importance of that tree's herbal, medicinal or magical properties, or some might just pick out a certain tree because of their childhood memories around that tree. After choosing the right material, you have to choose the appropriate shape and size of the runes. It is important to make sure that all the 25 runes can fit perfectly in the palms of the individual's cupped hands. The best measurements would be around 4 cm in length, equal to or less than 3 cm in width, and thickness of about 1 cm at most. When it comes to choosing the right shape, round runes are the most feasible to sculpt.

If you have chosen wood as your favorite material, then collect your favorite wood from the wild. Do not take more than needed. Be honest in your intent. Some people tend to pay the tree in silver coins as payment for giving them wood for the runes. They bury it under the tree. Since trees are also living entities, make sure to ask for their permission before breaking off a branch. Also, don't forget to show your gratitude to the tree.

After bringing the branch of your preferred tree, chop it into 25 equal pieces of the same dimensions. Removal of the tree's bark is not mandatory. You can clean it depending on your personal preference. Those who do not want to chop a tree's branch can buy dowels from a nearby hardware store. Though their options get limited, there are chances that they might come across their choice of wood in the dowel. Some of the most common options available are - pine, oak, and ash.

Rune symbols can be inscribed by carving into the wood with a sharp object or painting the symbols, or drawing on them with a felt-tip pen. Though carving and painting require a lot of effort, they are usually preferred since the more effort you put into making your runes, the more you get out of them.

Some people can paint effortlessly, while some shiver when they pick up a brush. Acrylic paints are the best option for the former ones as they can easily dip their brush into paints and draw the runic symbols on the wooden pieces. Those who cannot paint but want their runes to look like the painted ones can paint using markers. These markers easily work on wooden surfaces, and you will feel like you are using a felt-tip pen. These paint markers are available in a large variety of colors.

Some people also use stains on their runes. The key to using stains correctly and effectively is choosing a shade lighter than the wood you have selected. Stains have their disadvantages, too, and tend to change color once painted and might not look as desired. Sealants and varnishes are also among the other options you can choose. Varnish seals all the material's pores, and the owner is unable to touch the natural wooden surface. Though it gives a sheen to the wood, it makes it look unnatural and seals all the wood's energies. So, all the actual properties you see tend to get lost, and the runes look all plastic.

Always make sure that there are no marks on the reverse side of the medium. Any kind of identifying marks can lead to bias. Ensuring that there are no marks on the reverse side ensures that when the runes are turned face down during selection, a biased selection based on marks is not made. So, it is important to make sure that you do not decorate or leave any kinds of identification marks on the back end. But, if your runes are round-shaped, it is helpful to paint a simple line on the rune's reverse side that will indicate the North-South axis of the rune.

After gathering all the tools needed to craft runes, make sure to take a moment and realize their importance. Try to focus and understand that important work is being performed, an ancient tradition is being brought back from ancient times, and you are about to be more in control of your own life, surroundings, and world. Take a moment to show your gratitude, to realize the significance of rune making. You are not just making some tools, you are making friends that will provide you with a lifetime of guidance. Take a moment and meditate when you start sculpting runes, pray to your God, who has been your source of guidance until now. This whole moment might sound like a simple little thing, but this one tiny moment can actually elevate your menial woodshop project to the level of a holy ritual.

People belonging to any religion can use runes. Whether you are Christian or Pagan, monotheistic, or a worshipper of several different gods, you can always take the help of runes. But whichever or whatever faith you follow, it is important for you to realize and fully accept that the runes and the runic system, and the entire reality of the Norse people, accepted the concept of polytheism, i.e., the existence of multiple gods and forces at a single time in every dimension.

The personal feelings and thoughts of a person learning the runic system regarding the religion should not interfere or bother with how these gods and forces have inundated the lives of the runic system followers. The true power and the effectiveness of the runic symbols can truly be understood and increased by a thorough understanding of the Norse people, their special gods, and the crucial place that runes hold in their community. You can experience the feel for the surrounding atmosphere in which the rune lore was first practiced only through true and deep understanding and not just knowledge of the runic system. You can gain the ultimate benefits of following the runic system from this.

Odin and Freya were the patrons and guardians of the runes, and many runic system followers pray to these two for aid and knowledge. If we talk in Christian terms, we can take Odin as an equal of Jehovah since that is his status in the Norse pantheon. To understand Freya, you can envision her as the principle of growth, development, and light embodied beautifully in the arrival of the spring and its bursting out in its full form. Rune practitioners worship these two since they aim for personal maturing and evolution, not only in the material world but also in the spiritual world.

Runes practitioners need to learn and remember that runes have been both tools for magical change and divinatory powers for the longest time. The conversion from the Pagan ways to the new Christian ways took far more time than most historians have alleged and want us to believe. You cannot just believe that the transformation took a short time.

Ruling classes or the topmost tier were the first to adopt the new faith because they found something that benefitted them politically. On the other hand, the working class retaliated by changing their old ways since they didn't find anything advantageous in changing their beliefs, so they tried to hold on to them. The majority of the community, the backbone, and the peasant society held fast to their already present beliefs.

Iceland was the last country to change its faith. They held onto their old faith until the 11th century. The Old Faith lingered longest there. Even if today someone visits Iceland, they will encounter a large thriving community following the Pagan culture. If someone truly wishes to see, observe and learn the runic traditions, Iceland is the best place to visit. In Iceland, the living tradition of runes survives until date.

When carving your runes, try to make the best use of this moment and concentrate on your ambitions. Think of your short and long-term goals. Pray to Odin and Freya if you want to, and try to make a connection with them. They will surely guide your soul in making the perfect runes. The prayers will definitely help you to get over any kind of fear and will help you to embrace the procedure fully.

As a new student, you might be stuck, might not have the courage to step into a new beginning. At that time, Odin and Freya will provide you with strength. You might feel afraid of the woodwork because you have never used the tools before to do such work or might be afraid of ruining your runes due to the lack of painting skills. Don't let your fears consume you. Just like any artist doesn't start their artwork without picking up their tools, you cannot make your runes without starting with the woodwork.

If you are frightened of woodwork, soapstone is an excellent material for you. It is used extensively in the jewelry industry and is readily available in the market. They can be easily engraved on, you just need to use your creativity and imagination in the right way. You can use small metal pendant disks available in the markets, especially at fairs. They are easy to engrave and paint on, and you can always remove the paint if they don't like your previous work. It gives you the option of correcting your mistakes. The whole concentrating in the moment process will give you the best results, and it will all be worth the effort.

Color

After dividing the wood into twenty-five equal pieces, try to sand off the rough edges so that they look presentable. The time to paint the symbols of the runic system has come. You can pick any color of your choice to give your rune a personalized look. The more you put thought into choosing the runic material, the more connected you will feel to the runes. If you are confused by the color options, you can always go with the traditional ones. There are a variety of traditional colors that can exert a magical influence on the runes and the owner's subconscious.

The most used traditional color for rune magic is red. The color Red represents the active male principle, the force of life embodied in the color of blood. The color blue is also vastly used in runes since it represents Odin. The color is usually used by practitioners who pray to Odin for his blessings. Blue is also a color of healing and, therefore, a good option. Green is the color of the Goddess and represents prosperity, fertility, and growth. It is an ideal color for followers of Her - the Goddess. Female rune magicians especially prefer green.

It is totally okay if you do not want to choose any of the traditional colors. Do what your intuition tells you. It is your personal rune set, and it should be painted with colors of your personal choices.

Pouch

To make sure that you don't lose any rune pieces, it is advised to keep them in a pouch. They not only help you to maintain all your runes in one place, but they also simplify the process of transporting them from one place to another. The pouch needs to be big enough to hold all the twenty-five runes. It is advised to carry a pouch that is made of natural material, just like the runes.

Some of the options available to the runic followers are fur, linen, and cotton. Your pouch can be as simple as a cotton bag or as elaborate and decorated as a pearl wallet. It totally depends on its owner. Some people like to put effort into decorating their pouch, while some like to keep it simple. It also depends on the amount of time you can dedicate to making your pouch.

You can make a simple leather pouch with vertical slits at the top to allow a thong or cord to be passed through and drawn tight. If you are making a cloth pouch, always allow an extra inch at the top. Always make sure to sew as close to the edge as you can. This ensures that your pouch has plenty of room for the drawstring. Make sure to make a slit so you can run the drawstring through to the outside.

Red is a good color for your pouch since it has positive, vibrant, and magical vibes. Also, always remember that tradition should not dictate your choices. Your intuition should be making such big decisions, just like in the case of colors of paint for drawing runic symbols, so use your intuition to choose a color for your pouch. You can also decorate your pouch with embroidered symbols, tassels, bells, or anything that matters to you and has a very special and strong significance for you.

Rune Cloth

A rune cloth is a simple white cloth used by rune magicians to spread their rune pieces at random. The white cloth is the most ideal and suitable option because it is a universal symbol of purity and truth. It also provides the advantage of being totally neutral, which is the most important quality for a rune cloth. A rune cloth must be free of all distractions. There should not be any kind of prints or designs on the cloth. It shouldn't be very elaborately decorated or highly ornamented. These measures help avoid the mind and eye from getting distracted and help to focus on just the runes.

The cloth could be of another color also, but it should always be plain and simple. The material for this rune cloth doesn't need to be exceptionally procured. You can use any plain cloth, soft or harsh and old or new. The main aim of the cloth is to keep the runes clean.

To charge your runes with your own energy, try to keep them closed as often as possible. Your personal vibrations will get imprinted on the runes and will make them more personalized. The rune pouch can be worn on the belt, carried in the purse, or even be held in your lap as you read a book or watch TV. Always try to position it on your solar plexus region. The solar plexus region is located approximately between your diaphragm and your navel. It is important to place the rune pouch at this place because it is the energy center of the human body, and in this region, the person's aura is strongly felt. You can even put the pouch under your pillow before sleeping. You will see the advantages of this process very clearly. You will find that this method will bring you the added benefit of significant dreams, often on runic themes. The runes do not need to be in your contact 24*7 but at least a significant amount of time. You should make a genuine effort to attune the runes to your own personal 'wavelength' before making any serious actual divination attempt.

A Rune Cloth

This is a piece of fabric where you place the runes while doing a reading. Typically, a rune cloth is white and not too big. Do not worry about getting an exquisite and expensive piece of cloth for the rune casting just because you read somewhere that rune casting is a magical and exotic idea. The cloth is only to prevent your rune stones or crystals from becoming dirty. Dust is a deterrent in rune casting and any other reading, so the cloth helps keep the runes clean.

CHAPTER 11: RUNE PREPARATION AND STORAGE

Do you want your runes to work as efficiently as they did when you first made and used them? Then you need to take good care of them, but unlike taking care of other kinds of accessories, maintaining runes does not just entail cleaning them the orthodox way. It involves cleansing and charging them.

Note that runes can be powerful tools, primarily when you treat them with care and respect. You will need to cleanse and empower them, especially if they are still new or many people have already touched them.

One thing to remember is that runes are private and personal items, and their owners should be the only ones who keep and see them. You can place them on your desk or in your workspace. It could also be somewhere near your bed.

By keeping them close, you are letting them tune into your personal energy, leading to clearer and more concise rune readings. If you are using them often for reading other people, you will need to cleanse them more often.

Cleansing

There are many ways for you to cleanse your runes. You can choose whatever takes your fancy, but the most important thing is you do it often and regularly. Cleansing is even more important between uses or when you accidentally surround them with another person's energy for too long. Here are ways to cleanse your runes so they can work properly once again:

- Laying them out at night or early in the morning and leaving them out for at least 24 hours.

- Smudging - This method involves passing them through the smoke of smoldering herbs that contain purifying properties primarily designed to cleanse them. If you live somewhere where even a small fire can make your neighbors panic, you can substitute the herbs for a white candle.

- Using natural flowing water, you can also cleanse them using natural flowing water, like a creek or a nearby stream. Never use tap water for cleansing as it has gone through numerous treatment processes, but if you have a bit of rainwater saved in a container in your home, you can use that instead.

Empowering Yourself

When you continually work with your runes, you will gradually learn more about nature's power. You will understand your place in the universe, allowing you to experience growth in all aspects.

Nature teaches you about maintaining balance and being in harmony. By regularly communing with nature and the elements within, you cannot help but feel enlightened. You feel empowered, as well. Do it regularly, and you will find a true connection with the universe.

Aside from communing with nature, you can also wear runic symbols on your person to empower yourself. Runes give out powerful vibrations that can serve as protection against harm. They will attract their specific qualities toward your life. Wearing a rune around your neck, like a talisman, will subject your entire being to it and all its related influences.

If you just bought or made a new set of Runes or have been using it for a while already, you should consecrate it first before using it again. Aside from re-energizing your rune set, it will also make your readings more uniform and accurate.

Consecration means to make something holy. When you consecrate your runes, you turn them from regular stones or tiles into sacred tools for divination.

The great thing about runes is that you can re-consecrate them infinitely. If you realize that your readings have become less clear or accurate as of late, then you will need to consecrate them as soon as you can. You also have to do the consecration if you have not used your runes for a long time and they do not work like they used to anymore.

One thing to remember about consecrating runes is that you are not just purifying and preparing them for use but also creating a spiritual link between them and you. It is the reason you need not be a psychic to use runes. The runes themselves will serve as the bridge between you and the divine.

If you know how to read the runic symbols, you become an interpreter of the divine. You can use them to gain guidance from the other realms in the universe. When you cast and read them, you will discover that they tell a sort of story. You will discover patterns and trends you can use to figure out your next best course of action.

By consecrating your rune set and yourself in the process, you are helping yourself to open up to the messages/story hidden in the runes. It is true whether or not you use them for yourself or if you like to give readings to other people.

Even though you do not have to be a psychic to read runes, your perception will increase. It will increase so that you will know the answers even before you cast your runes. Every time it happens, keep track of everything that pops into your head regarding the reading, then check later if they confirm any of your earlier thoughts.

Now, on to the actual consecration process. Just like cleansing, there is no one method of consecrating runes. If you follow the basic requirements, then you will be fine.

First, you will need purifying smoke. Most heathenry practitioners use sage as its smoke has purifying qualities. Some people do not like sage as the smell of its smoke can be overpowering. If so, for you, then you can use incense. For consecration, you cannot go wrong by choosing traditional frankincense and myrrh.

But if you are not a fan of fragrances, you can use a white candle instead. The warm light given off by the candle can also serve as a catalyst. Choose whatever method works best for you.

The following are the basic steps for the basic consecration ceremony:

- Light the bundle of sage/incense and allow the smoke to flow over you and purify yourself and the container of your runes.

- Hold your runes using the non-dominant hand. Hold it over the sage/incense smoke or the flame of the white candle. It should be just high enough over it that you feel no pain.

- Seek your deity's aid for protection and protect your runes from all, save for the highest forms of energy.

- Look at each run and connect with them one by one. Imagine your energy going into each and becoming one with it. Now, with your non-dominant hand, hold them all again and place them over the smoke.

Ask your chosen deity to consecrate them so you can use them to help yourself and others.

After cleansing and consecrating your set, you can use it immediately. Keep them in a lined box or soft pouch when not in use, so they remain sacred and safe.

Empowering the Runes

You can empower your runes simply by keeping them close. You can do so by always carrying them in your pocket or bag. Another way to do it is to keep them within your personal space. That way, they can tune themselves to your personal energy.

Here are other tips you can use:

- Place them outside so the sun can bless them - Leave the runes outside at the crack of dawn, then bring them back into your home just before dusk.

- Bury your rune set into the soil - You can either bury them in one single pile or put them in a pouch and then bury them. You can dig them up after at least a week has passed.

On the other hand, you can also perform a small but intricate cleansing ceremony. First, cast a circle to chase away any negative energy, then cleanse the space and you use the smoke from a smoldering pile of sage. Lay down your casting cloth in the middle of the circle and your runes for cleansing.

Bless the runes with the elements. In this part, you can choose whatever has meaning for you. For instance, for the earth element, sprinkle rock salt. Pass them through the smoke of the sage for the air element. Sprinkle rainwater over them for the water element.

Finally, pass them through the flame of a lit red candle for the fire element. After you finish with the elements, hold each rune tightly in your right hand to imbue each with your spirit.

If you usually use the runes to guide others, it is best to cleanse them before and after every use. Also, it is advisable to re-empower your runes every full moon.

Consecrating Your Runes

After cleansing, it's time to consecrate your runes.

- Start by anointing yourself on your third eye, throat, and heart with a few drops of sacred oil or water.

- Anoint each rune with a touch of the same. Intone the runes as you do this, and feel their presence strengthen and become clearer and brighter.

Charging Your Runes

You can charge your runes as frequently as you'd like. You should certainly do so before your first reading, but you can also charge them whenever they need a little freshening up.

To charge your runes:

- If you are working with crystals (optional), arrange them around your runes so they point inward.

- Ground yourself and take a few deep breaths.

- Use your wand or finger to point at each rune in turn and trace its shape, simultaneously intoning its name or sound while focusing on its meaning and mystery.

- Repeat this process until you can feel the magic emanating from your runes.

When your runes have finished charging, place them in their pouch (you may want to cleanse and consecrate the pouch, as well) until they are ready to be cast for the first time.

Creating Sacred Space

A ritual environment is not necessary for the runes to work. It is for your benefit as their reader. The runes are ever-present and always whispering, but your mind is not always silent and ready to hear their wisdom. Conducting your readings in a sacred space will help quiet your mind to hear the whispers, prepare your consciousness to make the necessary connections, and remind you that divination is not a tool to be used on a whim. You must incorporate the wisdom you glean into the actions of your daily life, and that takes time and effort. If you are unwilling to dedicate time and effort to your reading, how can you commit to elevating yourself to the level of the wisdom you receive? Make sure you will not be disturbed or distracted during the reading, and give yourself plenty of time. The space can be indoors or outdoors, but it should be free of clutter, and you should be able to hear your own thoughts. Consider including music, incense, candles, essential oils, crystals, and plants in your rune rituals and readings.

It is best to use the same space and basic elements for most of your runework. If you do it in the same setting every time, context-dependent memory will make it easier for you to slip into an oracular or magical mind-set. You can, however, change certain details to fit your reading. Light particular candles or bring different crystals or talismans to the reading, depending on the topic. Experiment as spirit calls you, and over time you will find the balance between ritual repetition and situational tailoring.

Prepare for a Casting

Before you get settled into your space, make sure you have everything you need. Candles? Lighter? Jacket, shawl, or blanket? Pen? Moisturize, hydrate, and relieve yourself *before* you begin the ritual so you're not going in and out of sacred space during the reading or distracted by your own discomfort. Dress for the occasion. Put on a rose quartz necklace or your favorite lipstick before you look into your love life, or pour yourself (and any spirits present) a glass of the good stuff before you and the runes start talking money. You may also want to cast a circle around your rune-space.

A traditional setup includes an altar placed physically below the seated reader, such as a low table, but there are lots of options, so make yourself comfortable. Make sure you have ample space and a place to journal while the runes are still out. Lay out your casting cloth, and arrange your talismans, journal, and anything else you require according to your intuition. Place your rune pouch in the center of the casting cloth, and light any candles or incense. If you'd rather diffuse oils, that works, too. Call upon any spirits you wish to invite. When the space and the vibe feel good, close your eyes and take a few deep breaths.

As you inhale, feel the air clearing your mind, heart, and body. Feel your breath oxygenating your blood and awakening your mind. Exhale distractions, doubt, fear, and tension. If you wish, sing an offering of your voice to the runes: A simple intonation will do, or you could chant the rune names. Your voice serves to center your body in the setting of the reading and to greet and introduce yourself to the runes in the ritual context. Ground yourself by imagining that your feet and your spine reach like tree roots into the earth. Try to feel the earth's heartbeat. Feel the sun and moon activating the crown at the top of your head. Open the palms of your hands upward so you are ready to receive. When you feel settled, it's time to begin your rune casting.

The Proper Way to Store Your Runes

You can store your rune set in a bag, preferably made of a natural material. You also may use any pouch you fancy. You can place them in a wooden box.

Most rune casters use casting cloths, and it is common to find them paired with a particular rune set. If you will be using a casting cloth, it is best to stay consistent with its color and material when switching cloth. Doing so will let the runes get in tune with the casting cloth and vice versa. Like the runes themselves, you should also regularly cleanse the item you store because it is essentially their home.

CHAPTER 12: READ THE RUNES

How to Read Runes

Reading of Runes is very popular when it comes to divination because interpretation must be made in an effort to bring healing and meaning to the life of the person seeking divination intervention. Any of the alphabets from the different categories of Runes may be used in the practice as it is entirely up to an individual, but Elder Futhark seems to be the most popular, for the probable reason that it has the highest number of letters. That said, a common procedure that is used in the reading of Runes is:

- **Step 1**- Gather your Runes in a pouch, close your eyes and concentrate on the result that you want, whether for a past, present or future situation. Once you have come up with an answer, choose a rune from the pouch with your eyes closed.

- **Step 2** – Toss the Runes out of your pouch onto a soft surface as you think and meditate on the answer you want for your situation and with your eyes closed. Once you are sure of what you want, open your eyes and check out the Runes. Whichever appears to be the most outstanding at the first instance is the answer to your situation.

- **Step 3**- Lay the Runes on a grid, close your eyes and pass your hand over them as you concentrate your mind on what you want for an answer. If you are left-handed, use your right hand and vice versa. If your mind is on it, you will definitely sense the rune that carries your answer.

- **Step 4**- In a neutral state of mind, close your eyes and with all your Runes in a pouch, draw out three of them and put them in a line. Open your eyes and read the answers for your past, present and future situation according to the arrangement of the Runes.

Using any of the steps outlined above, choose two Runes and place them together. Depending on the meaning attached to each. They will either complement each other or work in opposing forces against each other. If they carry the same meaning, for example, they will support you tremendously but if they oppose, it means that one thing will happen followed by the other. They can also represent what needs to be fixed in a given situation.

You can use any of the steps outlined above to read Runes for your body mind and spirit. Select three Runes and place them next to each other. The one on the left represents your physical answer, the one in the middle of your mental state, and the one on the right your spiritual answers. To make a reading for dwarves, select four rules and place them in a circular shape so that you have one to the left, right, top and bottom. The rune at the top will give you answers relating to your past desires, the right one answers related to present desires, the bottom one answers to your innermost secret desires. If the desire is positive, it usually will manifest itself within four months.

You may also wish to read a layout composed of five Runes. The arrangement would be like that of the four rune, with one placed at the center of the circle. The interpretation would be that the rune at the bottom would represent the influences around your life question, the rune at the far left would represent the problems surrounding the question or problem, the rune at the top represents positive factors that surround the problem, the rune at the far right represents the most logical answer to the problem while the rune at the middle points to the future influences that surround the problem or question.

Sometimes you may want to do a reading that gives you more insight into your life. Using any of the steps above, choose five Runes and place them in a straight line next to each other. The rune to the far left will give you answers to your current situation, the one-second left one will reveal what is in your thought process at the present, the center one will reveal your current heart desires, the one next to the one at the center will reveal your focus in life while the one to the far right will reveal the influences you might encounter in future.

If you come across a runic cross layout in the process of seeking answers, the interpretation will be that the rune to the left of the cross represents past situations, the one to the far right represents future situations, the one at the center represents positive outcomes and the one beneath it represents present situations. The rune at the top represents the closest answer to your problem while the one at the bottom represents factors influencing the question or problem.

Rune reading should not be a complicated affair especially if you understand the different interpretations and meanings attached to each rune.

How to Write with Runes

Although Runes are a traditional alphabet that dates back to the 1<u>st</u> century AD, their mysticism and links with divination mean that people today are still interested in writing special messages using Runes. One particularly popular use for written Runes is tattooed, where people attempt to write out their names using Runes, or to create a cryptic message that will in some way determine their destiny.

Runes are not the same as a typical language, and therefore, the familiar rules of writing Runes do not apply. For example, in typical writing, one may substitute letters of similar alphabets to write a word for ease of translation. If you do that with Runes, you will create a word that has no meaning, or that cannot be adequately translated.

The main difference that occurs when one chooses to write with Runes is that the language is phonetic in nature. Therefore, when creating words, you need to write down what they sound like, rather than writing down the word based on the way that it is spelled.

Consider writing down the English word Sing in Runes. The sound S is represented by the rune named Sowilo. Then the sound I is represented by Isa and finally the sound NG is represented by a single rune (rather than N and G separately) which is known as Ingwaz. Therefore, the final word in Runes could be spoken as Sowilo Isa Ingawaz.

While this example is relatively straightforward, there are still interesting challenges that arise when one attempts to write in Runes. The main challenge is the change that has occurred over time in language. The sounds that are in use today are different from those that were in use centuries ago, and therefore, when it comes to the transcription of modern letters to Runes, there can be some difficulty.

When you want to begin transcribing, you should begin by jotting down the word in English. Following this, you should change the word into phonetics, and then you can alternate the English letter or sound with the appropriate rune.

You Should Use This Simple Guide to Get the Sounds and Letters Right:

1. Fehu represents the letter F, as it sounds in the word fish.

2. Uruz represents the letter U, as it sounds in Undo or the OO in the stool.

3. Thurisaz represents the letters TH, as they sound in

thorn.

4. Ansuz represents the letter A, as it sounds in apple.

5. Raido represents the letter R, as it sounds on the radio.

6. Kauno represents a hard C or a K, as the C sounds in the clock and the K in the key.

7. Gebo represents the letter G, as it sounds in grape.

8. Wunjo represents the letters W and V, as the W sounds in wind, and the V sounds in viper.

9. Hagalaz represents the letter H, as it sounds in happy.

10. Naudiz represents the letter N, as it sounds in new.

11. Isa represents the letter I in short, as it sounds in sing.

12. Jera represents the letters J and Y, as they J sounds in joke, and Y sounds in yak.

13. Ihwaz represents the letter I in its long-form, as well as instances of the letter Y, as the I sounds in the silo, and the Y sounds in style.

14. Perth represents the letter P, as it sounds in pork.

15. Algiz represents the letter Z, as it sounds in zebra. It

can also represent the letter S, as you would find in the word cousin.

16. Sowilo represents a soft C or the letter S, as the C sounds in lice, and the S sounds in see.

17. Tiwaz represents the letter T, as it sounds in the tree.

18. Berkanan represents the letter B, as it sounds in bail.

19. Ehwaz represents the letter E, as it sounds in elk.

20. Mannaz represents the letter M, as it sounds in the mail.

21. Laguz represents the letter L, as it sounds on the lawn.

22. Ingwaz represents the letter NG, as a compound consonant ng, as it sounds in linger.

23. Othila represents the letter O, as it sounds in orange or pot.

24. Dagaz represents the letter D, as it sounds in the doll.

There are certain pointers that you should take a note of when preparing to write in Runes. To begin with, you will realize that there are only 24 Runes, whereas there are 26 letters in the English alphabet.

In addition, there are several letters in the English language, which are silent, meaning that they do not add any value based on sound. These should be ignored or removed when changing the words to Runes.

Letters, which are repeated, such as you would find in the word nappy, do not need to be repeated. A single p can be represented and will comfortably suffice. In ancient writing, Runes did not have spaces, nor were they separated by punctuation marks. Modern writers use some spaces to help with the separation of words.

When writing in Runes, you should also consider the direction in which you write your words. For easier legibility, writing from left to right is recommended as this mimics modern English. If you are referring to the ancient text, you may find that the writing went in either direction, which can make interpreting a message quite interesting.

How to Make Your Own Set of Runes

With all the knowledge you have now about Runes, you may decide to look for them to have your own set. It may be a challenge to find exactly what it is that you are looking for. For that reason, it helps you to know what you need to do to create your own Rune set. When you create your Runes, the accuracy of your readings will improve dramatically. This is because you put some of your power into the making of the Runes.

The set that you choose to make will depend on what you want to use the Runes for and the materials that you have available to you. The most common materials used include stones, wood, and clay.

Choosing the Right Rocks for Your Runes

The best rocks for Runes are those that are smooth and soft enough to easily carve out, such as those that you would find smoothed up on a riverbed. So, to begin, you need to look for small rocks that are close to being the same size. Then you can customize these stones.

Choose a color that you like, which will help you to better connect with the Runes. Using this color, paint your chosen rune onto the rock. To avoid the paint from rubbing off, you need to add a protective coating or find another way to seal it.

Creating Runes Using Wood

You may not live near a river or a lake where you can easily find smooth stones. In that case, you need to use a different material, and an excellent option is a wood. As it is malleable, it can take any shape that you choose and can easily be turned into tiles. The best tiles for Runes are those which are round in form, usually shaped into disks. The best Runes are created from wood that has been shaped out of a branch that has fallen.

With stones, you need to paint on the marks for the Runes, but with wood, you have more flexibility. This means that you can use paint or choose to do a carving of the wood or event to use ink. To make the rune more attractive, you should stain the wood. The method you use to put the symbol on the rune will affect how the final staining is done. Natural wood can also be used for a rune, where there is no need to stain it.

Making Runes from Clay

This is a malleable material that allows you to mold the shape that you need for your rune easily. Once you have molded the shape, then you need to carve on the rune symbols. To ensure that they are ready, you will need to fire these Runes using a kiln. You will also find that you can be more creative with clay, coming up with various methods for decorating them.

Runes Made from Bones

The bones of animals are excellent for the creation of Runes. The issue is that bone tends to be quite fiddly and difficult to work with. To carve on bone and create the Runes, one needs to have some skill in this area. Otherwise, the Runes will easily get chipped and damaged.

Crafting a Rune Set

Crafting a Rune set will help one get more accurate readings since the Runes will be connected to the caster.

The choice of material is up to the crafter. While oak wood is best, it can be anything from stone to clay to shells. Some are easier to work with, but others might be more spiritually significant to the crafter.

After the material has been decided, it needs, of course, to be acquired. Stones and shells should be flat and rounded (preferably tumbled) and similar in size and shape. The easiest way to cut tiles from wood is to find a fallen branch and slice it into tiles. Whatever the material, make sure that it is legal to harvest it from an area. Don't forget to make an offering to the spirits of the land. In the case of wood, it is better to opt for a fallen branch as the wood from a living tree should only be cut when there aren't any other available sources. The offering you make should be safe for both the flora and the fauna of the area.

Deciding how to write the Runes is the next thing to do.

Modern ways include wood burning, painting, carving, or inking. To empower the Runes even further, blood can be used to tint or mixed with other pigments.

After the Runes are drawn, they should be consecrated. The methods differ from region to region, but the majority of Rune casters agree that they should be consecrated after being made.

The ritual space should be prepared, cleansed, and smudged. The Rune caster then invokes the Rune deities, ancestors, and other spirits they may want to present. The Runes are then laid out on a cloth that will be burned afterward. The Rune crafter offers a drink to the deities and then finally asks them to lend their powers of purification.

The Runes are washed, not soaked, in pure consecrated water. Another smudging blend of purifying herbs is then burned and dedicated to the deities. Then, each Rune is passed through the smoke while its name is spoken aloud and returned to the cloth.

Using a brush or quill, the Runes are painted or tinted (if carved) with the pigment of your choice. While each Rune is painted, its name is chanted. After all the Runes are painted or tinted, the sacred space is taken down, and the Runes are allowed to dry under cover.

After the Runes have dried, the sacred space is erected again, and the pigment sealed with a sealant of choice. While the Runes are being polished or sealed, a galdr should be sung to them.

After sealing, the Rune crafter holds each Rune over their heart and connects with them.

Layouts

Rune casting can be referred to as a 'layout' or a 'spread.' A spread is more like a tarot card reading, whereas a layout is the more classic way of casting. In my experience, there is very little difference between the two and it is really just whichever one you are comfortable with. Being that they are so similar, we will just call it a layout here and look at the different types that way.

One Rune Layout

Obviously, the first type of layout is a one rune layout. For this, as with all of your casting, you will be beginning after you have cleared your mind and relaxed. Now you will need to bring forth the thought or issue that has been concerning you previously and concentrate on that and that alone. If you want the runes to help you with it, you will have to be sure that you are leaving it out there to be dealt with.

For the one rune layout, reach into your pouch (or box) of runes and draw one out, or you can cast them and pick a single tile after. Whichever way you choose, this rune will represent the attitude attached to the question for which you seek guidance. You can also read it as the answer to this question.

This will be a broad answer, as you are only reading one rune, but try to remain patient and stick with this outcome. Casting more tiles or trying for a larger layout will only result in confusing the reading and it will be a lot harder to know if what you were given came to fruition. Try and remind yourself that the larger layouts will come with time and that the answer you were looking for was there, you just have to look for it.

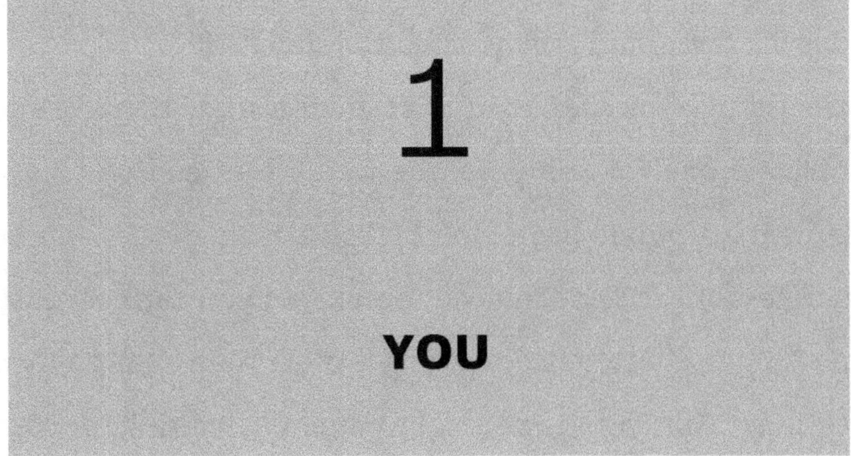

Two Rune Layout

Again, this may seem basic, but for beginners, East is more than sufficient. The Germanic people believed that time was split into two parts, "what is happening now" and "what is yet to happen," so the two rune layout is perfect for this concept. The past will come into play in our three rune layout, but for now, this is just fine.

When you cast your runes, the first one that you choose will allude to the present, and your suggested answers, attitudes, and solutions will be here. The second tile will be your "what is yet to happen," and as you begin to settle on the reading of the cast, it will help you to decide how to act going forward. Remember to intuit the runes as you see fit. Do not try and overthink it, as the answers are specific to your life force, and they will read as such.

Even though you are only using two runes, and therefore do not have one for the past, the first rune read will have elements of what has come before attached to it. These energies will accompany the present, so you can rest easy knowing that a two rune casting is more than enough for a beginner. Take your time and be patient in waiting for your answers to come.

12

YOU

Three Rune Layout (Past, Present, and Future)

Some practitioners do not agree with the two rune system, believing that there must be at least enough runes to cover the past, present, and future specifically. This is a matter of personal choice. I do believe that starting with three will be a little overwhelming to a beginner, but if it is the way you want to go, then that is up to you entirely. Those who wish to practice with one or two at first, then that is just as well. With the three rune layout, we now have a definitive past, present, and future. The first rune you cast (or pick, if casting several at once) will be on the left and will represent the past. It will show you the influences and choices that affected the question you have asked. This will allow you to learn from your past mistakes and avoid repeating them.

The second rune, placed in the middle, will represent your present. This will be a bit harder-hitting, as it will help you to realize the actions and emotions that are currently affecting or causing the issue that you have brought into question. Becoming aware that there is something we are doing or saying that is causing us pain or anxiety can be a bitter pill to swallow, but once we understand what those things are, then we can at least begin to do something about it.

Which leaves the third rune. This will be placed on the right and it will show us the outcome of our question. Reading the casting will allow you to interpret not only what you have to do to change how the situation turns out, but the suggested approach and attitude with which to undertake your journey of enlightenment and wholesome divination.

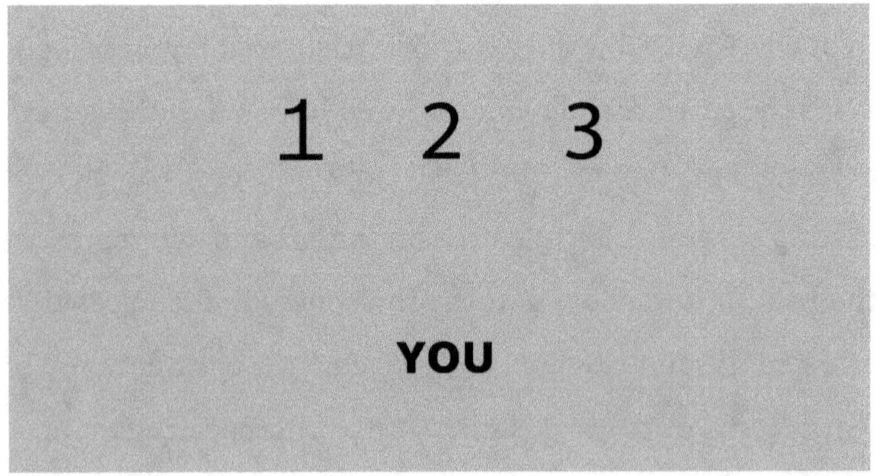

Four Directions Layout

In Norse mythology, we are told that the giant skull of Ymir is held up in the sky by four dwarves, named Nordri (north), Sudri (south), Austri (East), and Vestri (west). This giant skull was considered to be the sky above us and therefore extremely important. When we think of the fundamental directions mentioned, then we can see why this layout is so powerful.

The final layout of each rune after casting is, of course, north, south, east, west, so the placement here will bring no confusion. What will be different compared to our previous layouts is the addition of an extra rune after the threefold concept of time as we know it. Again, we need to let ourselves embrace the open-mindedness of our ancestors and allow the restraints of what we have been told to believe to slip away.

Nordi, or north, in this particular layout will be representative of the past. What came before is always important, and as much as we sometimes do not want to look back over old digressions or painful memories, it is essential to our progression in rune casting and our growth as human beings.

Looking to our rune on the west, or Vestri, will show us our present. Whatever question that you have brought to the casting and the answers that you seek, will be heavily influenced here. Always remember that the Elder Futhark is here to bring out the positive energies in our lives, so any negativity felt will only be fleeting, and the good will always shine through in the end.

Austri, or east, will not so much show us what is to come, as the third rune usually does in the layout previously, as that is reserved for Sudri. What it will do is help you to identify the issues and obstacles that may arise down the line. Although you will need to intuit from an array of emotions, they will all be connected to the single question that you have laid down, so do not worry about becoming overwhelmed.

With our fourth rune to the south, Sudri will be an interpretation of the other three runes combined, in a sense. This will be more so your 'future' rune, as it will be the one that helps point you in the right direction. Where Austri will help you to recognize the dangers that may befall you, Sudri will be the one that suggests the solutions.

An important thing to remember as we move past layouts of more than three runes is that oftentimes there will be a sort of odd one out. This is inevitable with several runes, and as the numbers grow, the opportunity for this to happen increases. Please do not worry though because your more complicated castings will only coincide with your growing experience. When there is a rune that doesn't quite seem to fit with the rest of the reading, then all you need to do is widen your perspective and take it all in as one.

These skills will come with time, and it is actually when we don't try so hard that the readings become easier. Looking for an exact answer will never work, so leaving your mind open to the energies that the Elder Futhark has to give is mainly about that aforementioned, 'belief.' Put your trust in yourself and the readings and divination will become a lot easier to interpret.

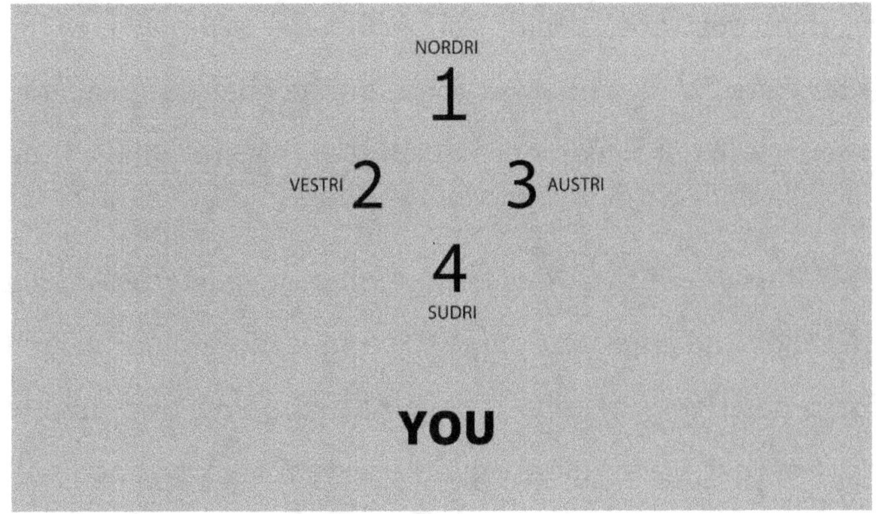

Five-Rune Cross Layout

The five rune layout, or "cross layout," will involve you picking five runes from your casting and laying them out on your cloth in a plus sign. As with all readings, regardless of how many runes you feel comfortable with, your reading will boil down to how you choose to take it. Many runes may seem like they will bring just as many conflicting answers, but the result will always be the same.

Once you have chosen your five runes, you need to place the first one in the middle of your plus, the second on the left (west) of this, the third on the top (north), the fourth goes on the bottom (south), and the fifth rune on the right (east). Our first rune represents our suggested answers to the simple influences and causes to the question that we have brought forward. What you get here will need to be interpreted as a whole, as some of the energies that you receive will not make sense until all of the runes have been read.

Thirdly, we will have the rune that suggests beneficial methods and emotions apply to the question in our search for a positive outcome. It will not give you one precise answer that will suddenly make everything okay, but it will guide you in the ways that you need personally at that time.

When we read our fourth rune, its strengths are in helping us to figure out some of the possible outcomes that our new focus will bring. Many of these will contrast, but that is only to show us that there are many paths that we can take, we just have to pick the one that suits us best.

Lastly, our fifth rune will bring us closer to the path which will suit us best. Having so many different aspects to one single question may seem like a lot, but trust me when I tell you that there can never be too many. They all add up to the same wondrous outcome, and that is enlightenment, open-mindedness, and fulfillment.

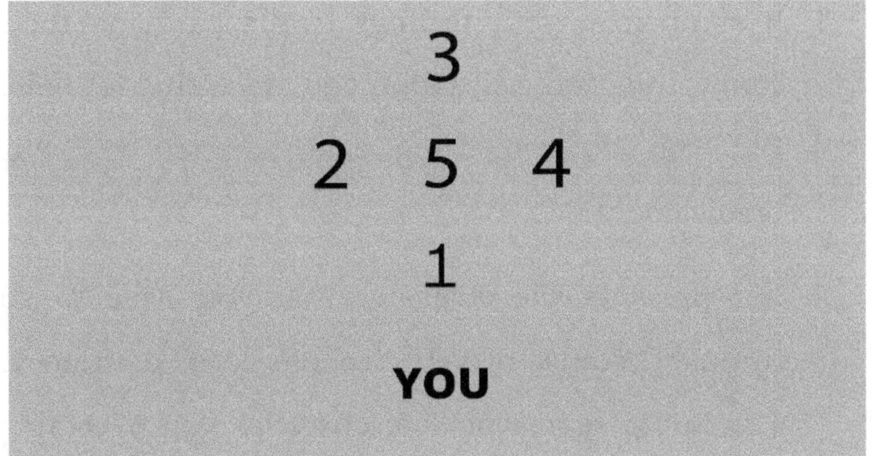

Midgard Serpent Layout

This rune layout is based upon Jormugandr, the gigantic serpent known to encircle the world. Legends say that Jormugandr is so huge that he can wrap his body around the earth and bite his own tail.

This is symbolic of how you need to be completely aware during the reading, or else the results of the layout might pass you by.

You will be setting up the seven-runes in a flowing pattern and imagine walking from the tail of the Midgard serpent up to its head. There will be a couple of uphill sections where you will be experiencing obstacles. However, note there will also be downhill sections where you can relax, making it possible for you to prepare yourself for the next uphill battle.

1. It symbolizes your feelings in the past and their connection to the situation you are asking for help. Did you do something that resulted in your predicament?

2. It represents the struggles that you have to go through because of your feelings from position 1. The hump represents the obstacles you overcame and that you need to know how you handled the past situation because it might come back to you in the present.

3. This point represents your feelings about your

situation. It is the rune nearest to your position because it roughly represents the present.

4. It is the position where you start on your journey toward your desired outcome. The obstacles from the previous positions may come back to you. The hump at this position is also much steeper than the one at position 2, meaning the obstacles you need to face are more difficult than before. However, you now have guidance from the past to help you.

5. It is the peak of your journey where you can see your goal. This rune will show you your feelings and how they can control you when you think that your goal is within reach.

6. It is the position that will remind you that there is still a bit more work to do before you reach your goal. You need to take heed of this rune the most. If it is telling you you need to put more effort, then do what it says. For instance, if you happen to cast a rune of power and control, you must be strong-willed and control your emotions until you reach your goals.

7. It is the Midgard Serpent's head, and most of the time,

it is the final goal. However, according to Norse mythology, Jormugandr could bite its own tail, so it is crucial to be mindful of what the runes are saying. Otherwise, you may find yourself back on the tail of the serpent.

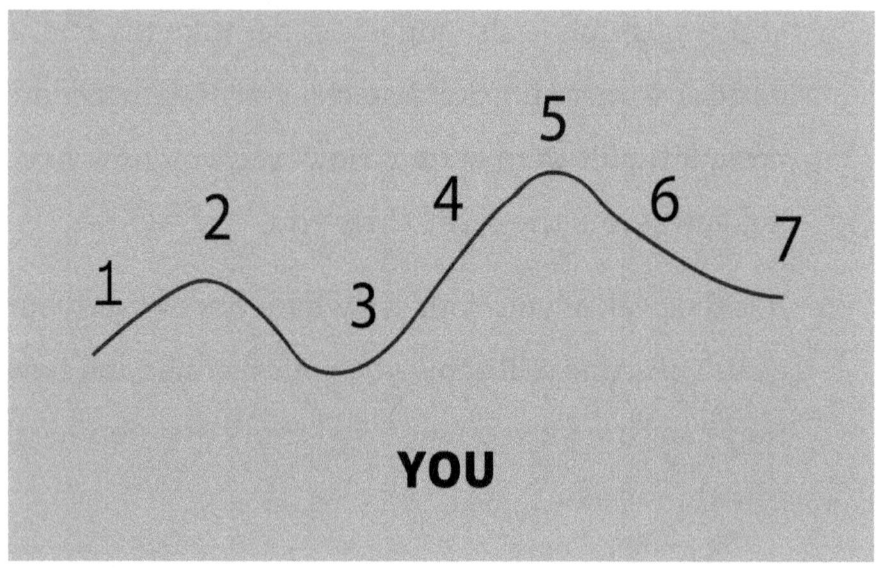

Bifrost Layout

According to Norse legends, the Bifrost is the rainbow bridge that connects Midgard, the realm of humans, to Asgard, the realm of the gods. By using this layout, you will be getting a sense you are getting help and guidance from the gods themselves. You will be casting seven runes and place them in an arcing pattern, starting from the left to the right. At the start is the color red, and it will end with the color violet.

- Red – It encompasses your attitudes from the past that might have some effect on your inquiry.

- Orange – It represents the effects of the past that result from your past attitudes.

- Yellow – This rune represents your attitude at present with an effect on your question.

- Green – It represents the effects of your current attitude on the overall outcome.

- Blue – The rune represents what kind of attitude you need to have in the future.

- Indigo – It symbolizes the effects of the attitude in the future.

- Violet – It represents the overall outcome of your journey.

This layout might seem like a complicated one. However, if you examine it closely, it is still just a past, present, and future layout with a couple of exceptions.

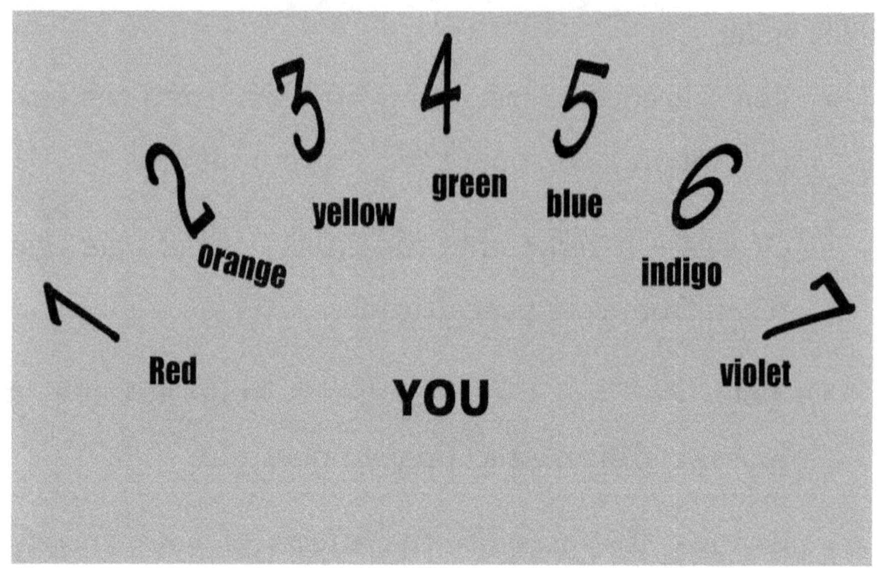

Grid of Nine Layout

The Grid of Nine requires that you cast nine runes and lay them out in a grid, like the one below. Ensure that you follow the numbering shown, as it plays an important role in the reading effectiveness.

The special thing about this grid is that if you add the values of any row or column, even the diagonals, you will always end up with an answer of 15. To read this layout, begin with the lowest horizontal row first. This row represents the factors from the past that influenced the matter at hand.

- 8 – It refers to the hidden influences that happened.

- 1 – It encompasses the basic influences you experienced.

- 6 – It represents your current attitude towards the events from the past.

You should then follow it up by reading the middle row from left to right, including:

- 3 – These are the hidden influences that are acting at present.

- 5 – It will represent the current status quo.

- 7 – It refers to your attitude toward the things happening in the present.

Last, you have to read the top row as it represents the outcome of your inquiry. It consists of:

- 4 – This refers to the hidden influences, the obstacles that prevent the outcome from surfacing.

- 9 – It is the absolute best outcome of your question.

- 2 – It will show how you respond to the result.

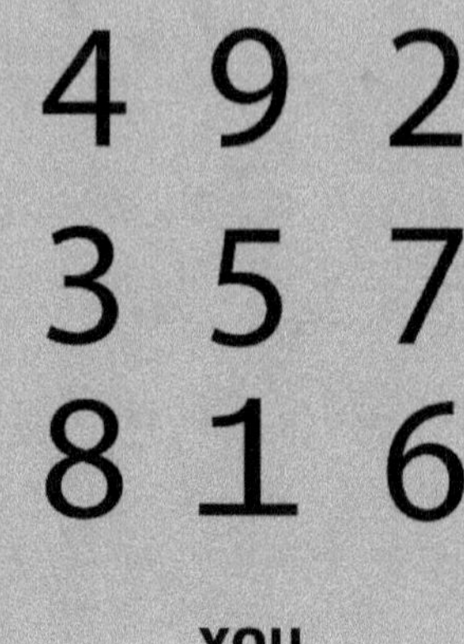

Odin's Nine Layout

Odin, the All-Father, hung from the branches of Yggdrasil to gain the knowledge of the runes.

The first six runes represent Odin himself (1 and 2 are the legs, 4 is the head), and the last three are for Odin's spear. To read this layout, follow this:

The runes in the first column (1 and 2) represent the factors in the past that might have influenced your question.

- 1 – It symbolizes the hidden images that happened in the past.

- 2 – It is your attitude toward the past.

The column with runes 3 and 4 represents the current affecting the outlet.

- 3 – It encompasses the hidden influences currently

happening.

- 4 – It is the questioner's attitude regarding current events.

The column with runes 5 and 6 will tell you about the answer to the question.

- 5 – This rune represents the hidden influences. It also symbolizes the causes of delay that may prevent the answer from manifesting.

- 6 – It is your response to the answer.

The last columns (7, 8, and 9) represent the powers you either have or have to deal with. These figures represent the powers you have to take care of for the first, second, and third columns, respectively.

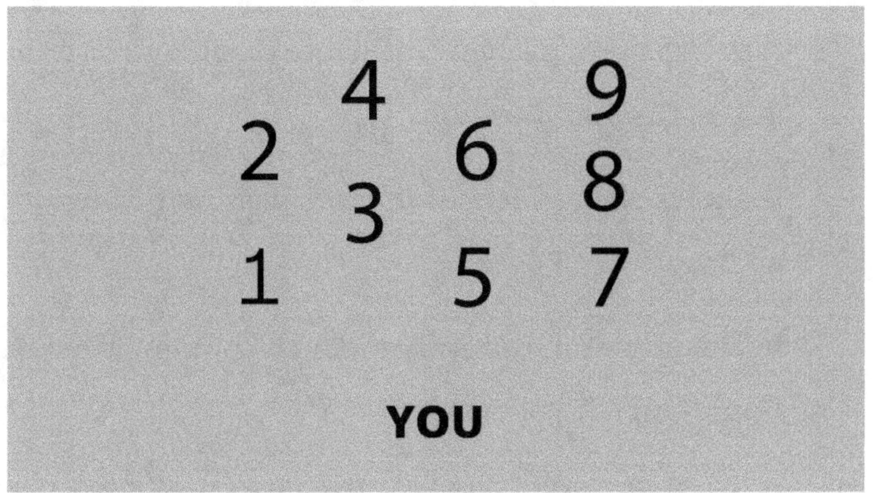

Celtic Cross Spread

Although this spread is usually used for tarot card reading, you can also use it for rune reading. You will need to cast ten runes from your pouch then lay them out in the same pattern as you would when reading tarot cards.

Before you cast, though, concentrate on the particular rune you would like help from. For instance, if you are trying to conceive, get a rune that represents fertility. Concentrate on getting it as you cast the ten tiles needed for this layout. If possible, place rune number 2 over number 1. To gain an understanding of this rune spread, here is how to read it:

1. This represents the question at hand.

2. It signifies the forces that might oppose your question.

3. It covers the underlying influence that may affect the answer to your question.

4. It shows the influences you are passing through or ending.

5. It encompasses the influences that might become important in the long term.

6. It represents the many influences you may come

across soon.

7. It refers to the fears and negative thoughts you may have.

8. It points to the outside influences that can potentially influence the outcome.

9. It refers to your beliefs and hopes.

10. It will provide the best outcome for your inquiry.

This layout may seem a bit complicated, so to make it easier, imagine Odin standing in front of you with his spear held by his left hand.

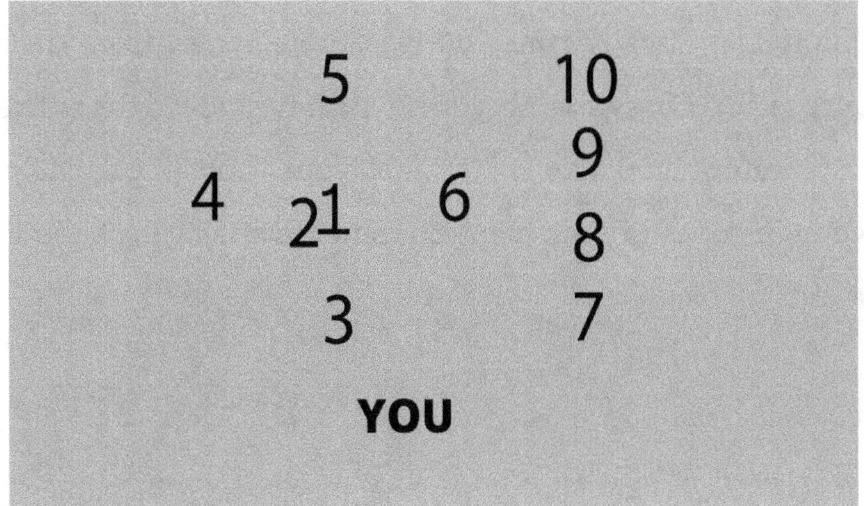

Egil's Whalebone Layout

This rune layout took inspiration from the Icelandic saga "Egil's Saga," which is about a master poet, warrior, and runemaster, and his many accomplishments. There is a chapter in the saga wherein Egil cured Thorfinn's daughter Helga from an incurable disease. The reason Helga was sick in the first place included the wrong runes placed on her head. Egil removed the erring runes and replaced them with the new ones he carved into whalebone, instantly curing her.

For this layout, you will be doing something that differs somewhat from the other readings. Instead of each rune having a different meaning, you can group them by threes and read as if the group is speaking. It is basically a three-rune spread but doing them four times in one layout.

The four groups of runes derived their names from their purpose in the saga. Now, you do not have to read the entire saga before you can use this layout, but it can help. Knowing the story can help you remember what each group stands for.

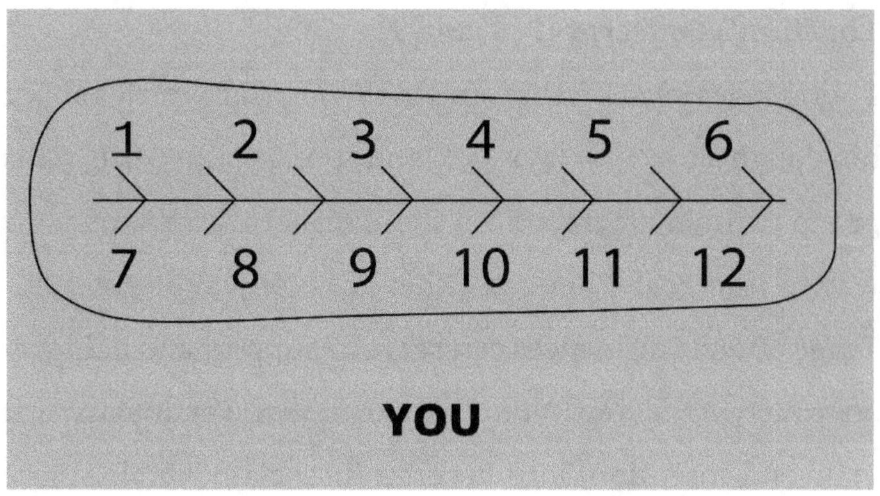

Carver's Intentions (1, 2, and 3)

In the story, the rune carver had specific intentions for the runes. The first group acts just like that. You have a certain intention you want to consult the runes for. Before you cast the first three, think hard about what answers you want them to show you. Keep this intention in mind while picking out those that you intend to use. You need to keep this intention in mind while you are working towards the answer.

Helga's Results (4, 5, and 6)

Helga is Thorfinn's daughter, and she is the one harmed by the errant runes placed upon her forehead. For your purposes, this rune group will let you see the wrong results that could manifest if you have impure intentions or do not intend to put effort toward your goal.

Thorfinn's Concerns (7, 8, and 9)

Thorfinn is Helga's father, and in the saga, he worries about his daughter as she lays sick and dying on her bed. This group of runes is symbolic of the external concerns on your way to your goal. They can either be helpful or disruptive.

These outside influences can serve as support and help you on your way toward your intended goal. For instance, if your end intention is to become financially stable, these outside influences may come in the form of family and friends who help you when you are down in the dumps or help you find a more stable and higher-paying job.

The outside forces can also have a negative effect and may even hinder you from reaching your intended results. Using the example earlier of becoming financially stable, the outside forces may be your family or friends with ridiculous spending habits. They are influencing you to make irresponsible spending.

This group of runes will show you the things you need to keep an eye out for. Such could be helpful or destructive, and it will be up to you to discern which is which.

Egil's Results (10, 11, and 12)

Egil is the runemaster in the story. When he saw the runes, the state that Helga was in, and Thorfinn's concern for his daughter, he still made everything right again. Through his masterful skills of manipulating runes, he undid the previous rune maker's damage and made Helga healthy again.

This does not mean you need to recast your runes until you reach your desired outcome. This last set of three runes will only teach you how you can overcome the things you previously learned to achieve your goal. It also does not mean you can just disregard the previous three groups. It tells you how you can still reach your goal while remembering the possible difficulties that came from the first three groups. Think of the first three rune groups as a heads-up as to what you can expect on your journey so you can prepare yourself for the challenges.

The neat thing about rune layouts is that you have a choice whether to stick with the traditional ones (the one, two, three, or four rune layout) or make up your own. If you do the latter, make sure that it at least makes sense to you. The most important thing is that you use your insight to decipher what the runes are telling you based on the circumstances of the person asking the questions and the possible definitions, as stated by the runes themselves.

CHAPTER 13: THE IMPORTANCE OF COSMOLOGY AND NUMEROLOGY

The ancient Nordic people did not see the cosmos as only the Earth surrounded by the heavens above and the underworld or hell below. According to Asatru, the cosmos was a complex system of multiple realms and planes, including the human realm. All these planes of creation were interconnected with each other.

Before the start of time, Muspelheim, the fiery realm of fire, which was in the south, moved north to meet Niflheim, the icy realm. They met at Ginnungagap or the yawning void, and their powers combined.

Nine realms are existing in Norse cosmology. The center of their universe and what connects all the realms together is situated in Asgard, and it is known as Yggdrasil, the World Tree.

The story from the **Völuspá** poem describes the events that took place during the creation of all things.

Two great realms once existed: one of ice and one of fire. They were separated by a terrible void called the Ginnungagap. These realms were to be known as Niflheim and Muspelheim, in turn. From the eventual collision of these realms, the ice on Niflheim melted and revealed Ymir, the proto-giant, and a cow called Audhumla.

Now, Audhumla licked away at the ice and uncovered Búri, the forefather of the gods. Audhumla and Búri sired son Borr and daughter Bestla, who in turn sired the brother gods known as Odin, Vili, and Vé. Flesh for the earth, skull for the sky, bones for mountains, and blood for sea. The World Tree emerged soon after the world's creation along with all the many beings and realms. Once it was all done, with the help of God Baldr, from the deep woods emerged the first two humans, named Ask and Embla, and they began populating the new realm.

The early Norse works of Eddic and Skaldic poetry assumes the reader has knowledge of cosmology, and thus, not much explanation is given on location and specific characteristics. Although Snorri's work of the nine realms changed it slightly adding and removing realms to include Helheim, or Hel (the Underworld), there is an importance of understanding that in Scandinavia at the time these descriptions would probably not be recognized and be quite different. Theirs was a living dynamic faith, and our knowledge is but just the surface of a much larger iceberg.

Yggdrasil, the World Tree, is thought to be the center of the Norse universe. The origins of the name have various sources, but it is generally understood as 'gallows' in Old Norse.

Situated in the realm of Asgard, upon its roots live multiple creatures and beings: the dragon of death, Níðhöggr, the four stags Dáinn, Duneyrr, Dvalinn, and Duraþrór who eat at the branches and roots, and the great unnamed eagle. Below the roots lies the Serpent of the World that chokes the roots surrounding Midgard. The tree has three roots that feed on three different wells: the Well of Urd in Asgard, the Well of Mímir by the frost giants, and the Hvergelmir Well in Niflheim.

But most importantly we see the connection to the three Norns: Uror, Verðandi, and Skuld. Their purpose is to nourish the World Tree with water from the sacred Well of Urd to prevent it from dying, and to twine the threads of fates of all things, often thought to be the roots of the tree themselves. They are secretive and unseen, rarely revealing their fateful secrets to men. They could be malevolent or benevolent, often determining the future of newborn children.

The primeval cow licked the ice and created a new being named Buri, and from Buri came Borr. Marriages among these early beings, as well as sexless reproduction by Ymir, resulted in multiple generations of beings until three godly beings, namely Odin, Villi, and Ve, killed Ymir and created the cosmos from his body parts. The cosmos created from Ymir's body parts consisted of the World Tree and the Nine Worlds. The World Tree, Yggdrasil, supported the Nine Worlds, who were separated by vast distances.

Ásgarðr

As it's been already mentioned, Ásgarðr was the home of the Æsir, who was a ruling race of gods that included Óðinn, Thórr, and Frigg. According to Sturluson, Ásgarðr was far more fertile land than any other and was blessed with abundant wealth, jewels, and gold.

An unfinished wall surrounded the realm. A master stonemason had offered to build Ásgarðr's surrounding wall in return for getting the Goddess Freyja as his wife, along with the sun and the moon. The gods agreed. However, they didn't know that the stonemason was a Hrimthurs giant in disguise. When they found out, Thórr struck down the stonemason, killing him and leaving the wall incomplete.

Ásgarðr is also where the hall of the slain, Valhalla, lies. Valhalla is a massive feasting hall that Óðinn rules over. In there, the dead who have been slain in combat, also known as Einherjar, are feasting and preparing to help the gods during Ragnarök.

Jötunheimr

Jötunheimr (Anglicized: Jotunheim) is the home realm of the giants (Jötnar). It is separated from Asgard by the river Ífingr and was said to lay under the second root of Yggdrasil, where Ginnungagap used to be.

Útgarðar (anglicized: Utgard) is the capital city of Jötunheimr and serves as the giants' stronghold. It's ruled by Útgarða-Loki (who's also known as Skrýmir).

The realm is described as eternally cold and deep in winter frost and rife with deep dark forests and high mountains. It was in Jötunheimr that Óðinn sacrificed one of his eyes to gain wisdom at the well of Mímisbrunnr.

Vanaheim

There is not much information on Vanaheim, apart from it being the home realm of the Vanir. The Vanir were associated with wisdom, fertility, and fortune-telling. However, following the war with the Æsir, the Vanir became a part of the Æsir.

In Heimskringla, Vanaheim is described to lay around the Don River (that used to be known as "Vana Fork"). It is also mentioned to be the realm in which the God Njǫrðr grew up.

Niflheim

Niflheim roughly translates as "Home of the Mist." Its location in the texts often overlaps with Hel, so it is possible that after its role in the creation of the world, the realm became the home realm of the underworld queen Hel.

Niflheimr was the second world created and was a frozen realm, which was home to the well Hvergelmir, from which all the rivers flow and the glacial rivers of Élivágar.

As stated by the "Prose Edda," a long time before Midgard was created, Niflheim existed, and inside there was a cave named Hvergelmir. In Hvergelmir were the springs of several venomous rivers that were known as the Élivágar. The names of the rivers were:

- Svol

- Gunnthro

- Form

- Finbul

- Thul

- Slid and Hrid

- Sylg and Ylg

- Vid

- Leipt

- Gjoll

After traveling far from their springs through Niflheim, they froze and hardened, becoming ice. This ice was what eventually rose out of Niflheim and battled over with the flames of Muspelheim.

Hel, the underworld goddess, was a daughter of Loki who was cast into Niflheim by Óðinn.

Muspelheim

Muspelheim was the first realm to emerge from Ginnungagap and was a world of raging fire. It served as home to the fire giants and was ruled by Surtr, who is going to be the one who brings out the fire that will consume the world in Ragnarök.

According to Gylfaginning in the "Prose Edda," the fire giants of Muspell will shatter the Bifröst Bridge during Ragnarök.

Alfheim

Alfheim, meaning "elf home," is the world of the elves. Alfheim is located on the highest level of the Yggdrasil, along with Asgard and Vanaheim—the realms of the Aesir and Vanir. The palace of the ruler and God Freyr is located in Alfheim. While not much is mentioned about the elves, as they tend to stay out of the events of Old Norse mythology, it is known that the light elves, or Ljosalfar, are seen as more beautiful than the sun, and considered guardian angels. They have the potential to help or harm humans with their magical powers of nature and fertility. The Dokkalfar, or dark elves, reside in Svartalfheim.

Niðavellir or Svartálfaheimr

Another realm that was home to a definite type of mythical Norse creature was Nidavellir. The Norse dwarves were believed to be master craftsmen and smiths who often worked with forges and in mines located underground. The

Dwarves were known to be quite secretive and busy in their work and this realm was also located beneath Midgard, under the ground. They could be found working in the caves or under the rocks as the realm was majorly built of stone. The name of the realm means "wane of the moon" or "new moon" in the Old Norse language.

The other name of the realm, Svartalfheim, translates to "Dark fields" as the realm was mostly dark and cold. The only light source came from the torches lit on the high walls and the forge fires that burned day and night. The fire created a lot of smoke in the realm that complemented its dark spirit. The talented craftsmen of this realm built several gifts for the Aesir gods, most of which are significant to Norse mythology, such as Thor's hammer, Mjolnir, and Odin's spear, Gungnir. Draupnir, the magical ring, was also believed to have been created by the dwarves of Nidavellir.

Helheim

As stated, sources aren't always clear about the nine realms, so while Hel was cast in Niflheim by Óðinn, there is also the mention of Niflhel, which was the lowest level of Niflheim, which might refer to Helheim.

Hel was given power over all nine worlds to allocate all dwellings among the dead that were sent to her: usually those who died of sickness or old age. Hel is said to be extremely wealthy, and her walls and gates are great.

The realm served as an afterlife for those who didn't die a notable or heroic death or that the gods felt weren't brave enough to join them later in Ragnarök. Unlike the Christian "Hell," the Norse afterlife was more a continuation of life in another realm rather than a place of eternal torment.

Midgard

Midgard is the world of humans: the Earthly realm. It sits at the trunk of Yggdrasil and is the center of the other nine realms.

Midgard is in the middle—in more than one meaning. Regarding innangard and utangard, Midgard has elements of both order and chaos. Midgard is also located between Asgard and Hel. The three are linear on Yggdrasil and are even connected. Asgard is connected to Midgard by a burning rainbow bridge called Bifrost that ends at Himinbjorg, the home to God Heimdall. Hel is connected through the graves that lead to the Underworld.

CHAPTER 14: THE POEMS OF THE GODS

The Eddas

The Eddas are a collection of two Medieval Icelandic manuscripts of mythology that use prose (stories) and poems in different stanzas to describe, depict, and detail the religion, cosmology, and history of ancient Scandinavian culture. The composition of the poems can either use the Eddaic or Skaldic genre of poetry and mainly uses alliterative versing and symbolism.

It is still unsure where the term 'Edda' derives from exactly, and there are quite a few hypotheses, but the easiest etymology to point towards is the Old Norse word *óðr* meaning 'poetry.'

The two collections of work are known as the Poetic Edda and the Prose Edda.

Poetic Edda

Just like the name says, the **Poetic Edda** is a book of poems that are all about Norse mythology. Most of the information in the **Poetic Edda** comes from two poems: "Völuspá," which means "The Insight of the Seeress," and "Grímnismál," which means "The Song of the Hooded One."

The poem with the most information about Norse mythology is "Völuspá." In this poem, Odin, the leader of the gods, goes to a wise woman and asks her to tell the future. To prove that she really does know what's going to happen, he asks her to tell him about the past. She doesn't know anything about Odin, but she is still able to tell him how the cosmos, in other words, the universe, was made (which you will learn about in the next chapter) and where the first dwarves, elves, and humans came from.

The **Poetic Edda** isn't easy for us to understand nowadays, but in the past, when people still believed in the Norse gods, it made perfect sense.

Poetic Edda, or Elder Edda, is a compilation of Icelandic and Norwegian tales that first appeared in the 13th century and is contained in the **Codex Regius** or "Royal Book." Many other poems were added to the Poetic Edda over the years and they were composed with visionary force and dramatic quality.

The Poetic Edda was more often written in an Eddic genre of poetry and follows these four rules:

- The author is anonymous.

- It uses a certain meterage (*fornyröislag*, *ljóðaháttr, and málaháttr*).

- It has a direct approach to word order.

- Kennings (ancient figures of speech) are used less.

By far the most extensive source of Norse mythology, the Poetic Edda consists of two separate parts: the Mythological Poems and the Heroic Lays.

The Mythological Poems tell us about the adventures of the gods from their own perspectives and carries eleven poems: Völuspá, Hávamál, Vafþrúðnismál, Grimnismál, Skirnismál, Hábarðsljóð, Hymiskviða, Lokasenna, Þrymskviða, Völundarkviða, and Alvíssmál.

The Heroic Lays, in three parts, depicts the challenges and journeys of heroes and heroines and carries nineteen songs:

1. The Helgi Lays consist of six stories:

Helgakviða Hundingsbana I, Helgakviða Hjörvarðssonar, Helgakviða Hundingsbana II, Helgakviða Hundingsbana I, Helgakviða Hjörvarðssonar, **and** Helgakviða Hundingsbana II.

2. The Niflung Cycle consists of fifteen stories:

Frá dauða Sinfjötla, Grípisspá, Reginsmál, Fáfnismál,

Sigrdrífumál, Brot af Sigurðarkviðu, Guðrúnarkviða I, Sigurðarkviða hin skamma, Heimreið Brynhildar, Dráp Niflunga, Guðrúnarkviða II, Guðrúnarkviða III, Oddrúnargrátr, Atlakviða, **and** Atlamál hin grenienzku.

3. The Jörmunrekkr Lays consisting of two stories:

Guðrúnarhvöt, Hamðismál.

Prose Edda

Snorri Sturluson, an Icelandic scholar, wrote The **Prose Edda**. A scholar is someone who knows a lot about a subject. Snorri knew a lot about Norse history and mythology. His book has a lot of the same poems and information as the **Poetic Edda**. He also added a lot of new information. Some of the poems in the **Prose Edda** are copied from older poems that don't exist anymore. Not all the things Snorri wrote down are true. He did make up some things and change the stories a little bit. Something you should always remember about some books is that not everything you read is true. People can write down anything they want, and sometimes what they write down isn't what really happened. Luckily, we know which parts of the stories Snorri made up. In this book, we tell the stories that Snorri didn't change.

The very first story you will learn, which comes from the **Poetic Edda**, is the Norse story about how the world started. In mythology, stories about the beginning of the world are called creation stories, or creation myths.

Prose Edda, or Younger Edda, is an Icelandic textbook written in the 13th century. Scholars assume that a large part of the text was written by law speaker and poet Snorri Sturluson. He was known for a verse use that was reflective of court poetry, putting him in higher esteem with peers.

Snorri Sturluson has long proven a paradoxical figure for those who think and write about medieval Norse culture. Many scholars believe that a satisfactory understanding of Snorri and his work will only be possible once the contradictions that surround this most famous medieval Icelander have been resolved. (Wanner, 2008)

The recomposing of stories altered the characteristics and influences of the gods in some writings but made them easier to comprehend.

The Prose Edda was typically written in the skaldic genre of poetry following these rules:

- The author is known.

- Ornate meterage is used (**dróttkvæt**t or a variation).

- Sentences are commonly interwoven and contain ornate syntax.

- Kennings are often used.

The Prose Edda consists of four sections:

- Prologue

- Gylfaginning

- Skáldskaparmál

- Háttatal

Magic and Poetry

Odin and Freya are the greatest shamans of the Norse gods. Shamanism is a form of magic in which practitioners can contact spirits or interact with the spirit world to accomplish a purpose. Odin is especially known for his spiritual-journeys, while his body remained in Asgard, appearing to others as if he was asleep. Such an instance is when he visited the underworld, on Sleipnir (an eight-legged horse attributed to shamanic trances) to find out what was Baldur's fate. As a practitioner of shamanism, Odin is surrounded by plenty of animal familiar spirits, such as his ravens, the wolves Geri and Fleki, and even the

Valkyries (even though they are maidens, they are still spiritual beings that serve the Allfather). The ritual of death and rebirth that Odin underwent to decipher the runes is also part of shamanic practice, if there was any doubt left regarding the god's abilities.

Shamanism is a part of the traditional *seidr,* the form of magic that was considered acceptable for only women to master - that is why Freya is a patron of it. Men who practiced seidr were scorned and even banished from society if the animosities ran deep. Odin's affinity for shamanism made him a target for ridicule and taunts. His 10-years exile from Asgard is said to have been in part due to his preferences in "doing a woman's work." To say that magic tarnished Odin's reputation would be an understatement. It questioned his honor and his ability to perform his "manly" duties. However, to Odin, the idea of honor was not everything, and he gladly discarded the concept if it meant he could indulge in ecstatic practices.

Odin's connection to poetry goes back to the time when he stole the mead of poetry, a drink made by the dwarves from Kvasir's corpse. Kvasir was the wisest man to ever live, and anyone who consumed the mead made from his body gained knowledge and the ability to compose poems. Of course, Odin was interested in possessing this mead, and he acquired it through trickery; by seducing the giantess who guarded it. But Odin, in an act of generosity, decided to share the gift of poetry with humans, gods, and other beings, making him a patron of scholars, poets, storytellers, and composers. To flaunt his poetic abilities, it is said that Odin only speaks through verses.

Rune Poems

Rune poems are the top source of relevance to the Younger Futhark's 16-letter alphabet. They provide their user an explanation of each runic letter in a poetic stanza to help them remember the pronunciation and relevance for each rune. Each of these rune poems has a couple of lines giving memorable images to help remember the name of the rune. They are divided into three parts: Norwegian Rune Poems, Icelandic Rune Poems, and Anglo-Saxon Rune Poems. Norwegian and Icelandic poems were based on the Younger Futhark, while the Anglo-Saxon used the relevant Anglo-Saxon Runic alphabet.

Due to the sheer amount of information on each region's version of the poems, we will provide the most well systematized of the three: the Icelandic Rune Poems of the

15th century.

Fehu

Money is a comfort to all men.

every man, though, must greatly deal it out, if he will before the Lord cast his lot

in favorable judgment.

Uruz

Aurochs is single-minded and over-horned, a very fierce beast – it fights with its horns – an illustrious moor-stepper;

that is a bold creature!

Thor

Thorn is awfully sharp, evil for any thane3 to grasp, unfathomably cruel

to every man who touches him.

Ansuz

A god is the fountain of all speech, wisdom's foundation and wise men's comfort

and every earl's ease and hope.

Raidho

Riding is soft for every warrior in a hall and grueling to him who sits high upon

a strong hard horse over miles-long paths.

Kauno

Torch is to each of the living known by fire, shining and bright; it burns most often

inside where princes are.

Gebo

Gifting, for gentlemen, is garnishment and praise, care and worthiness; and for every wretched outcast, blessing and life, who otherwise would be without.

Wunjo

Happiness has he who knows little of woes, sores, and sorrows, and for himself has fruitfulness and merriment, and also a town's security.

Hagalaz

Hail is the whitest grain; it whirls out of heaven's sky, storms' winds wheel it 'round; it turns to water after.

Naudiz

Need is narrow in the breast.

though often it turns for the sons of men

into help and into healing nevertheless,

if they listen to it early.

Isa

Ice is over-cold, unfathomably slippery.

it glistens glass-clear, just like gems.

a floor wrought by frost, a fair sight.

Jera

Harvest is men's hope, when God, heaven's holy king, lets the lands give

bright fruits to the rich and the needy.

Ihwaz

Yew is on the outside an unsmooth tree, hard, earth-fast, fire's shepherd,

underpinned by roots, a joy in its homeland.

Peord

Dice is always play and laughter among high-spirited, where warriors sit

blithely together in the beerhall.

Algiz

Elk sedge has its dwelling oftenest in marshland, it grows in water; it wounds grimly,

it bloodily burns all men who do any taking of it at all.

Sowilo

Sun to seamen always is hope, when they ferry it over the fish's bath,

until the surf-stallion brings them to land.

Tiwaz

Tyr is a token; it holds trust well with princes, on a journey, it is always

over nights' mists, it never fails.

Berkanan

Birch is fruitless; even so, it bears shoots without seed; it is

beautiful of branches, high of the crown, fairly decorated.

grown with leaves, it presses the sky.

Ehwaz

Horse is, for earls, noblemen's joy, a horse on proud hooves,

when men around him, wealthy ones on horses, exchange

speech.

and to the restless, it is ever a comfort.

Mannaz

Man, in mirth is dear to his kin.

though each one shall forsake the others,

for the Lord wills by his doom

that poor flesh to the earth be given.

Laguz

Sea is thought of as endless by men, if they should dare to

be in a tilting boat, and the sea-waves frighten them very

much,

and the surf-stallion cares not about its bridle.

Ingwaz

Ing was earliest seen by men among the Danes, until he later eastward

went over the waves; a wagon ran after him.

thus, hard ones named that hero.

Dagaz

Homeland is over-dear to each and every man, if there he

may enjoy, by right and in properness, fruitfulness at home

most often.

Othila

Day is sent by the Lord, dear to men, Method's illustrious

light, mirth, and hope

to rich and poor, useful to all.

CONCLUSION

Thank you for reading this book. Reading books on the Norse gods and the history of the Old Norse people should be a part of your path. The Norse faith comes with homework. Before you decide to embark on this spiritual journey, you should make sure you are ready for it.

As for the Nordic rituals, these too were packed with values to be learned by the people. The continuous sacrifices, for example, taught the tribes to give gratitude and never to take blessings, or even nature, for granted. Offering sacrifices also taught the pagans the fleeting value of material items, thus constantly re-targeting the people's attention towards their value as human beings, rather than letting them obsess over material possessions.

If a person wants to be connected with the power of the runes, they will need to know all of the history and mythology that goes along with each of the runes. This is crucial to make sure that you are getting the full, true meaning behind all of these runes.

While the history of these dates back to the beginning forms of writing, there is the issue that you need to make sure that you know that there are those that associate these with magic. Many people have the feeling that these offer a wide range of powers in helping to direct a person along the path that they are currently on.

Good luck.